# Foxtrot to Arihant
The story of Indian Navy's Submarine Arm

Joseph P. Chacko

Copyright © 2014 Joseph P Chacko
ISBN 13: 978-81-930055-5-2 ISBN 10: 81-930055-5-4
All rights reserved.

Published by

**Frontier India Technology**
No 22, 4th Floor, MK Joshi Building, Devi Chowk, Shastri Nagar,
Dombivli West, Maharashtra, India. 421202
http://frontierindia.org
https://www.facebook.com/frontierindiapublishing
The views expressed in this book are those of the author and not at all of the publisher. The publisher is not responsible for the views of the author and authenticity of the data, in any way whatsoever. Cataloging / listing of this book for re-sale purpose can be done, only by the authorised companies. Cataloging /listing or sale by unauthorized distributors / bookshops /booksellers etc., is strictly prohibited and will be legally prosecuted. All disputes are subject to Thane, Maharashtra jurisdiction only.

# DEDICATION

Dedicated to the Indian Navy Submariners.

# CONTENTS

Foreword (VAdm. K.N. Sushil (Retd)): 1
The Historical Perspective of Submarines (Cmde. Ranjit Rai (Retd.)): 4
Submarines in the Indian Context: 7
History – Conventional Submarines in India: 10
Foxtrots – The Kalvari Class: 23.
The Vela Class: 28
The Swedish Offer : 31
HDW Type 1500 – Shishumar Class : 35
877EKM - The Kilo - Sindhughosh Class : 45
The Indian Submarine Design : 51
30 Year Plan For Submarine Construction : 54
Project 75 – The Scorpene : 57
Submarines At War - 1971 : 68
Submarine Accidents : 80
Midgets and Chariots : 87
Nuclear Submarines For India – Historical Perspective : 92
Leased Nuclear Submarines – INS Chakra : 99
Indian Nuclear Submarine Project - ATV – Arihant : 119
The Untold Story of the Arihant(Cmde. Ranjit Rai (Retd.)) : 134
The SSGN's : 144
P-75 India : 148
Submarines – The Debates Within (Cmde Arun Kumar (Retd)) : 153
Submarine Rescue : 160
Autonomous Underwater Vehicles : 173
Submarine Command Structure : 175
Submarine Training : 179
Submarine Communication : 181
Submarine Support Vessel – INS Amba : 183
Key Submarine Bases and Infrastructure : 185
DRDO and Submarine Technologies : 193
Ex Brasstacks : When Pakistan's Red Submarines kept India's Blue Navy at Bay (Cmde Ranjit Rai (Redt)) : 199
Some Exciting Moments in Submarining (Cmde Arun Kumar (Retd)) : 205
The Submarine Arm Comes of Age (Cmde Arun Kumar (Retd)): 218
Future Indian Naval Submarines : 224
Technical and Tactical Data – Foxtrot , Chakra - Charlie-I, Shishumar, Sindhugosh, Scorpene, Chakra – Akula II & Arihant : 231
Abbreviations : 239
Index : 240

# ACKNOWLEDGMENTS

First and foremost, I am indebted to Cmde Arun Kumar AVSM, NM. (Retd), for his interaction and feedback on the book. He was very kind, enthusiastic, and pleasant to interact with. He sent a lot of new information and closed the gaps in the book. This book was not possible without his insights and guidance. He has spent 28 years in the submarine arm and had a distinguished career. His Bio merits a separate page and is available just before the author's page at the end of the book.

**Cmde Arun Kumar (Retd) runs "The Brave New World Foundation," a Public Charitable Trust set up to commemorate the memory of an exceptionally gifted and bright son, ALYOSHA KUMAR. As the publisher, Frontier India Technology is contributing 10 % of the net profits earned by selling this book in the first three years to the Trust.**
**I encourage others to visit the site and, if possible, donate:**
**www.thebravenewworldfoundation.com**

I thank VAdm K.N. Sushil PVSM, AVSM, NM (Retd) for his encouragement, Foreword, and other contributions to the book. Commissioned into the Indian Navy in 1973, VAdm Sushil joined the submarine arm in 1976. He was part of the commissioning crew of submarine INS Shankush as XO and later commissioned the first Indian-built SSK submarine INS Shalki as its CO. On promotion to the rank of rear admiral, he held the appointments as flag officer submarines at Visakhapatnam, assistant chief of Naval Staff (Submarine), ACNS (Special Submarine Project), and Project Director ATV (Operations and Training) at the Integrated Headquarters, Ministry of Defence (Navy). VAdm Sushil was the Indian Navy's first inspector general of nuclear safety. He retired as the Flag Officer Commanding-in-chief of the Southern Naval Command after serving the navy for 39 years.

I want to acknowledge Cmde Ranjit Rai (Retd). He is a National Yachting Bronze medalist, specialist Navigator, and IAF trained Air Controller. He attended Yarrow Shipyard, HMS Dryad, and RN Staff College in the UK. Commanded four ships and Naval Academy and served as Director Naval Operations and Intelligence DNI at Naval HQ New Delhi and Defence Adviser Singapore. The idea of the book was triggered while interacting with him. I owe a considerable to him as he allowed me to co-author the book 'Warring Navies – India and Pakistan,' which instilled confidence in me to write my books.

This book has been edited by Ravishankar Basavaraju, Akshitij Malik and Ritu Sharma.

# FOREWORD

*"Pitt was the greatest fool that ever existed to encourage a mode of warfare which those who command the sea did not want and which, if successful, would deprive them of it."*
**Earl Vincent**, First Sea Lord

Admiral John Jervis, 1$^{st}$ Earl of St Vincent, whose Naval Career spanned the American War of Independence, must have been aware of David Bushnell's submarine's attack (albeit unsuccessful) on HMS Eagle and pondered the strategic relevance of submarines. His denigration of William Pitt epitomizes the attitude and vehement opposition the purveyors of 'Sea Control' have displayed through the centuries against submarine warfare. This bigoted attitude is borne out of ignorance, incomprehension, and fear began to change only towards the close of the second world war. At this stage, the surface warfare clan dethroned the battleship and crowned the Aircraft Carrier as the queen of Sea Control.

The commissioning of INS KALVARI, the first "Foxtrot" class submarine in 1967, acquired from the erstwhile Soviet Union, was a milestone event in the history of Indian Naval acquisitions. This class of submarines based on German WWII design provided us with appropriate technology and safety features that enabled us to develop and establish a professional submarine operating ethos and tactical doctrines. The "Foxtrots" fitted in with the then naval tactical requirements. The constantly changing geo-political scenario, new maritime surveillance, and sensor technologies impose on us continually upgrading and adapting to these changes' challenges.

In the mid-eighties, the Government of India signed an agreement with the Federal Republic of Germany for what would infamously become the HDW programme. The strategic purpose behind the programme was to equip ourselves with indigenous submarine building capability. In the din and darkness of the scandal, we lost track, stopped indigenous construction, and continued acquiring Soviet Kilo Class submarines. Almost 15 years after delivering the second HDW submarine, MDL finds itself collaborating with DCN France in building the Scorpene class.

Conventional submarine capabilities have increased manifold. Air Independent Propulsion systems and torpedo tube-launched cruise missiles have drastically altered the submarine's underwater staying power and the area she can threaten. Still, batteries will continue to impose limitations if the submarine must sustain high speeds for prolonged periods. Modern conventional submarines, in our case, are ideally suited for operations on the Arabian Sea and the Bay of Bengal in a variety of missions.

We are a Nuclear power. For Nuclear deterrence to be effective, we must deploy an assured, survivable second-strike capability, which only SSBNs can deliver. France and England have decided that their Nuclear strike capability would be entirely SSBN based. Our Nuclear doctrine stipulates 'credible minimum deterrence.' Strategic planners must determine the number of weapons that would have to be deployed to give credence to our deterrence philosophy. That will also determine the number of

SSBNs that need to be built and deployed.

The arrival of the Nuclear submarine revolutionized submarine capability. The submarine now became the only platform that could independently threaten any land area or force anywhere in the world. This vital asymmetrical force multiplication capability allows submarines to be deployed in both sea denial and sea control missions.

SSNs are the only platforms that can be deployed covertly and, if required, signal their presence overtly to ensure deterrence. The Indian Navy needs a balance force mix of modern SSNs and SSBNs to give credibility to our policy of Nuclear deterrence under No First Use.

By **VAdm K.N. Sushil,** PVSM, AVSM, NM (Retd.)

# THE HISTORICAL PERSPECTIVE OF SUBMARINES

*Though the first submersible vehicles were tools for exploring underwater, it did not take long for inventors to recognize their military potential'.*
**Bishop John Wilkins** of Chester, in Strategic Advantages

The evolution of submarines recounts advances in seafaring. Watertight submersible boats and roundels with glass windows were lowered into waters with ropes for exploration. The first military submarine fitted with screws and propelled by pedals was the 'Turtle' in 1776, designed by David Bushnell in Britain and improved by Fulton in the early 19th century called 'Nautilus. Gustave Zédé built a 60-foot, battery-powered 'Gymnote' capable of 8 knots on the surface for the French Navy with ballast tanks and periscope. Still, he had limited underwater ability and no means for recharging the batteries.

The Germans invented a clutch between the steam engine and an electric motor, which functioned as a dynamo to recharge the batteries for underwater endurance. On the eve of World War I, the art of submarine warfare was new. Still, conventional diesel-electric submarines with torpedoes and guns on deck sunk more tonnage than surface ships in both World Wars, and the importance of submarines has only increased.

The year 1954 saw a breakthrough in America. The first miniature nuclear power reactor to produce continuous steam for propulsion under water-powered the USS Nautilus. Four years later, the Soviets scientists under Anatoly Petrovich Alexandrov constructed 24 nuclear boats in three classes, all with the same reactor, to challenge American aircraft carriers in the Cold War era. Today the pear-shaped hull nuclear submarines with long underwater endurance are fitted with vertical launched nuclear-tipped SLBMs. These are the best form of nuclear deterrence, and only five nations, the US, Russia, France, Britain, and China, have made and operated atomic submarines. Britain has leaned heavily on American technology and for Trident SLBMs for their nuclear submarines. With the launch of INS Arihant, India too has taken steps to achieve a deterrent.

## Submarines - Tactical and Strategic War Assets

Diesel submarines are warships of position, whereas nuclear submarines are vehicles of maneuver. Diesels are suited for small shallow seas near the coast, but nuclear propulsion is the desired choice when rapid movements over long distances are required. A conventional submarine needs to be in the vicinity of its target. The sinking of INS Khukri on 9th December 1971 by PNS Hangor off Diu with 178 naval souls going down displayed the power of submarines in war, and now for deterrence. Large maritime nations have to possess both conventional and nuclear submarines in their order of battle (ORBAT). The cost of building nuclear submarines is approximately 50 % to 75% higher per unit than diesel-electric powered boats but has greater capabilities.

A nuclear boat can be speedily dispatched to a long distance to intercept or track and only attack when ordered. The sinking of the Argentinean cruiser, ARA General Belgrano, in the Falklands by HMS Conqueror shows the capability of the nuclear submarine. She was dispatched at full speed for 8000 miles, submerged all the way. No conventional submarine could have achieved this, and the action bottled up the Argentinean fleet. Unlike the diesel-electric boats, which have to surface to recharge batteries about 20 percent of their time at sea, the nuclear submarine does not have to come up. In the atomic age, nuclear submarines provide nuclear deterrence, as was proved in the Cold War.

By **CMDE Ranjit B. Rai** (Retd.)

# SUBMARINES IN THE INDIAN CONTEXT

*"Submarines are an essential component of a sea denial strategy. They effectively exploit their stealth characteristics and the opaque underwater environment to interdict enemy surface operations using anti-ship torpedoes and missiles. They can also be used for ISR, laying mines, SF insertion and conduct of direct land attack, if fitted with land-attack missiles."*
*Book -* **Indian Defence Strategy, 2009**

The Asian region, especially South Asia to the East China Sea, is scrambling for naval expansion owing to the negative aspects of the regional power displayed by the People's Republic of China (PRC). By now, every small nation in the region understands that they should field a submarine force as a cost-effective solution for sea denial against a larger navy, and most of them are investing in the submarines.

India has explicitly described its naval expansion as a response to its rising economic profile and the Chinese naval buildup. Although the submarine count has become a weak spot in the naval equipment profile, India is engaged in upgrading its existing submarine fleet and developing and buying newer sophisticated ones. Nuclear propulsion, Air Independent Propulsion (AIP), conventional cruise missiles, and nuclear-tipped ballistic missiles are the emerging trends of Indian naval submarine strategy.

The nine 877EKM (Kilo) submarines form the backbone of the Indian Navy's subsurface combatant fleet. The other subs include the four HDW Type 1500 conventional submarines and one nuclear-powered Russian Akula II class submarine.

The Kilo submarines have been undergoing refits in Russia and India, with Indian equipment and Russian Klub cruise missiles for anti-ship and land-attack roles. Two of the Type 1500s are being considered for upgrades.

The first of the newly contracted and domestically built conventional Scorpene-class submarine is scheduled to be inducted by 2015- 16. The Navy has begun taking the indigenously designed SSBN INS Arihant through its testing phase on its eastern sea face.

Expected Indian submarine acquisitions include the Russian Akula II class and six submarines of the new P-75 India class. Two additional Arihant class are being built, and 6 SSGNs have been approved for construction.

Indian Navy estimates a requirement for at least 18 conventional submarines and 6 SSGNs to deter Pakistan and China, both of which are rapidly expanding their subsurface combat arms.

## The rationale for Nuclear Submarines

India traditionally has had a Continental outlook as a legacy of the Mughal reign. Before that, India had a glorious maritime tradition under the Gupta Dynasty, Satavahanas, Chalukyas, Zamorin, Marathas, and others. During those times, the Indian shipbuilding industry was renowned. Many of the ships of the Royal Navy in the 19th century were built in India. Now 95% of India's trade moves by sea, and the potential of its extensive Exclusive Economic Zone (EEZ) is tremendous. Protecting the sea trade and EEZ requires substantial naval resources to operate for a sustained duration.

As India began globalizing and economic assets are being acquired worldwide, it has become imperative to maintain a navy that can enforce the security of the assets. It calls for naval deployments for longer ranges.

The aircraft carrier vs. nuclear submarine debate becomes irrelevant as the Indian Navy is creating Carrier Battle Groups (CBG), which require underwater protection in terms of nuclear submarines.

Nuclear-powered fleets ensure a tactical advantage as they can be positioned well in advance of an impending conflict. Nuclear submarines at choke points can help both offense and defense.

The Indian Navy has grown to be a net security provider in the Indian Ocean region and requires a naval presence.

India also has a strategic intent for nuclear submarines. The Indian Nuclear Doctrine in Para 2.1 states, "India's strategic interests require effective, credible nuclear deterrent and adequate retaliatory capability should deterrence fail." Further, para 4.1 to 4.3 states that "credibility," "effectiveness," and "survivability" are the cardinal principles under which India's nuclear deterrent will function. The SSBNs meet the specific conditions of "requirements and responses" since they have the flexibility, survivability, and endurance required for the Indian decision-makers.

The Indian Navy plans to operate a minimum of five SSBNs and six SSGNs in the long run.

# HISTORY – CONVENTIONAL SUBMARINES IN INDIA

*"The Admiralty are not prepared to take any steps in regards to submarines, because this vessel is the weapon of the weaker nation. If, however, this vessel can be rendered practical, the nation which possesses it will cease to be weak and will become really powerful. More than any other nation we should have to fear the attack of submarines."*
**George Goschen**, First Lord of the Admiralty

Pre-independence, the Indian seamen and officers of the Royal Indian Navy (RIN) were trained in anti-submarine warfare (A/S), and since RIN did not operate submarines, target practice was always a problem. With the cessation of World War II hostilities and the inevitability of India becoming independent, the British began developing naval plans for the future Indian Navy.

Three naval plans were developed for India before the independence. A two-phased plan was prepared in April 1944 by Vice Admiral Godfrey, the Commander in Chief of the Royal Indian Navy, for submission to the Chiefs of Staff Committee. The Phase II of the plan envisaged the acquisition of aircraft carriers and submarines with associated training and maintenance facilities. The second plan, "The Chiefs of Staff Committee Report of 1944 on The Size and Composition of the Post War Forces in India," had no mention of submarines. But the third plan, "Committee for Planning the Requirement of the Armed Forces 1945," recommended submarines for defending Indian coastal shipping in the event of an attack from the United States of America (U.S), China or the Soviet Union, till the Imperial forces moved in for defence.

India became independent on 15th August 1947. The country faced formidable economic challenges, and financial allotment for military services was a lower priority. The Army and the Air force were given a significant share of the defence budget due to the immediate threat posed by Pakistan. The navy was viewed as the Cinderella service with little or no role in the military conflicts at the time. The navy provided ambitious plans for equipment but had to settle for far less.

In August 1947, a new plan, 'Outline Plan for the Reorganisation and Development of the Indian Navy," which was authored by Cdr. A.K. Chatterji, the first Director of Naval Plans, Lt. Cdr. N. Krishnan the Staff Officer Plans, and Lt. Cdr. Y.N. Singh, the navy's first aviator, proposed the acquisition of four submarines without specifying the acquisition period, as there was no information on the availability of the platform. Due to the budgetary constraints, the plans kept changing, and by 1951 the submarine requirement had dropped from the plan radar.

In 1956, Pakistan joined CENTO and SEATO, and the U.S. led Cold War efforts. As the American's and the British lent equipment and training assistance to the Pakistani armed forces, the Indian Navy began revisiting its plan to match the new scenario in the region. However, the submarines were not projected as a requirement.

The need to acquire a submarine was felt during the 1956 annual Commonwealth JET (Joint Exercise Trincomalee) exercises. The navy was dissatisfied with the inadequate availability of the Royal Navy submarine to practice the A/S maneuvers and approached the government.

In May 1957, Defence Minister Mr. K.R. Krishna Menon wrote to the First Sea Lord, Admiral Mountbatten for "acquiring a target submarine service comprising the oldest and cheapest submarines since it was not envisaged that India would need to employ them in war" ('Sea Power and Indian Security' by Rahul Roy Choudhary). The British found it difficult to loan a training submarine due to extended commitments, submarine shortage, and complicated procedures to lend the British naval personnel. Instead, the Royal Navy suggested more A/S training time in Indian waters, which was accepted by the navy.

The lack of practice submarines was again felt in 1958 when the navy received sophisticated ships with anti-submarine capabilities, and the case for a submarine arm was re-stated. Adm. A.K. Chatterji writes in his book 'Indian Navy's Submarine Arm, "A paper was submitted to the Government in 1959 for the acquisition of three operational submarines which would also naturally be available as target submarines for the anti-submarine ships. Protracted discussions took place with the Government at various levels over the years without much progress."

Budgetary constraints apart, the navy found it challenging to convince the decision-makers in India and Britain, as the submarine is considered an offensive platform. VAdm G.M. Hiranandani writes in his book 'Transition to Eminence: Indian Navy 1965-75', "The British were adamant in their views that submarines were sophisticated weapon systems which were difficult to operate, that the Indian Navy was still too young to venture into the submarine field, that submarines were accident prone, that the loss of a submarine at sea would lead to the loss of confidence in the Navy at Governmental and national level which would gravely impair the Navy's further development......

"Examples were quoted of the Australian and Canadian Navies which operated submarines on loan from the British Navy, manned by British personnel with a few junior officers and sailors as trainees......

"Having just attained independence, the thought of adding any warship to the Indian Navy commanded by a British officer and manned by British sailors was repugnant to Indian sentiments."

In the meantime, the British had moved on from the older Porpoise class submarines to the newer Oberon class with greater underwater endurance. The British had also loaned their A and T class submarines along with British submariners to commonwealth members Australia and Canada for training.

The navy continued to engage the government with the requirement. VAdm. Hiranandani writes, "It (the navy) impressed on the Government that every navy worth its name had to have submarines. It took several years to train an officer in the operation of a submarine and give him sufficient experience to ensure that he would be competent to assume command of a submarine. The navy urged that the Government accept the creation of the Submarine Arm in principle and allow the navy to depute a few officers to Britain for training in submarines."

In 1962, the government agreed to depute junior officers to Britain based on the Navy's argument that intimate knowledge of submarines would help better anti-submarine measures. At the same time, the government also made it clear that it was not committing to acquire submarines.

The first group of trainees headed to HMS Dolphin in Britain for submarine training in the same year. In the book "Blueprint to Bluewater, the Indian Navy, 1951-65,' RAdm Satyendra Singh writes, "The first batch of five officers comprised Captain (later Commodore) B.K. Dang, who was to later establish the nucleus of Submarine Arm, Lt. Cdr. K.S. Subra-Manian and Lieutenants M.N. Vasudeva, R.J. Millan and A. Auditto. These officers sailed for the UK in February 1962 for training on HMS Dolphin; Capt. Dang for a special condensed, acquaintance course of six months' duration and the others for one-year training in submarine operation. They were to study the infrastructure organisation, operational know-how and maintenance and back-up facilities required for setting up the submarine arm of the navy." Other than officers, the group had senior naval sailors from various trades. A second batch was also sent to the UK for training in July 1963. A total of 15 officers and 20 sailors were trained in the UK for submarine operations by 1965.

During the 1962 Indo-China war, the Indian military leadership perceived a combined naval threat from China and Pakistan. The Chinese People's Liberation Army Navy (PLAN) had 25 submarines, and twenty-one of these could operate in the Bay of Bengal and the Arabian Sea. While the reassessment of the Chinese naval threat ruled out a naval conflict but the presence of Chinese submarines had been confirmed, writes RAdm Satyendra Singh in the book

'Blueprint to Bluewater'.

After the war, the navy argued that the Hunter-Killer submarines had a role against the Chinese and projected a requirement for three submarines. One sub was required to be on patrol, while the second was in transit and the third under repairs or refit or resting of crew. The submarines had to operate 1500 miles from Indian shores for patrolling areas like the Malacca Straits.

By 1963, the navy listed four options to explore for the purchase of the submarines. The first option was to purchase the 20-year old A and/or T submarines from Britain, which Admiralty offered, and these submarines had a short life span. The second option was older American submarines which could be operated for five years after modernization. The U.S. was unlikely to give India the subs due to lack of mutual treaties and the fact that the ally British were the traditional suppliers of military hardware to India. The third option was British Porpoise or Oberon class. And the fourth Option was the new Russian F class which was similar to British Porpoise and American Fleet Class.

The navy finally decided on three British Porpoise class submarines, and in 1963 the Indian Government began negotiations with the British for acquiring a one-second hand Porpoise class submarine to begin with. As usual, the Royal Navy expressed its inability to spare its submarines. The British shipbuilders were willing to build a new Oberon class submarine, but Britain refused soft credit, and India had a foreign exchange shortage.

On 20 April 1964, Mr. Y.B. Chavan, the Defence Minister, told Pressmen in Bombay that the government was keen on giving training to Indian navy personnel for crewing submarines. The acquisition of submarines depended on the availability of foreign exchange. He admitted that the navy occupied a "low priority" compared to the army and the air force. 'This did not mean, however, that they were neglecting the navy," he said.

India also approached the U.S. for the submarines. An Inter-Service Defence delegation headed by Defence Minister Y.B. Chavan and the Deputy Chief of Naval Staff Commodore (later Admiral and CNS) S.M. Nanda as the senior service representative visited the U.S in May 1964 for discussions which included acquiring two or three Fleet class submarines. It was the time when the U.S feared losing Pakistan altogether to China. The U.S. govt advised the delegation to go back to its traditional suppliers, the British. The U.S. govt's impression of the Chinese naval threat to India was also not in sync with the Indian apprehensions. It was then the Indian govt decided to approach the Soviet Union for the submarine requirement.

The September 1964 talks with the Soviet Union were positive as the Soviets agreed to supply four F-class submarines and a submarine depot ship. The delegation returned without signing any agreement under the instructions of the government. The book 'Transition to Triumph: History of the Indian Navy, 1965-1975' by VAdm. Hiranandani quotes Adm S.M. Nanda "When we came back, I got to know what had happened. It appeared that the instructions had come from the Government, who had been influenced by the British and the American Governments, that the Navy should not go in for Russian acquisitions. And so in 1964, we did not take the Russian submarines that were being offered to us."

Mr R.D. Pradhan from the Indian Administrative Service, who was the Private Secretary of Defence Minister Mr Y.B. Chavan from 1962 to 1965, writes in his memoirs 'Debacle to Revival', "Lal Bahadur Shastri (the Prime Minister) felt that before making any commitment to the Soviets, the Defence Minister should visit Britain to find out the attitude of the British Government. Apparently, the situation had become favourable with the advent of the Labour Party in 1964 under Prime Minister Harold Wilson".

A delegation left for Britain in November 1964. The new government appeared sympathetic, but the Royal Navy parroted its usual inability to give up its submarines. However, this time they offered a T-class sub which was meant for scrapping. Indians counter offered to take the T class as a loan till an Oberon class could be provided.

After Royal Navy's refusal, the British Government offered an Oberon class submarine. So the Indian delegation placed the order for an Oberon class submarine on a deferred credit of Rs. 5 crores. However, the offer was withdrawn by the British.

The outcome of the visit was published by the Kabul Times on 21st November 1964 on its front page. Quoting Reuters, the news item stated, "Britain pledged continued aid for India's defence build-up including the provision of a Royal Navy submarine for a period each year for anti-submarine training. The British aid was announced in a communique at the end of government talks with an Indian Defence Mission led by Y.B. Chavan, Defence Minister, on military assistance for India's five-year defence programme. The communique said Chavan had indicated that a modern submarine was required to increase the anti-submarine capacity of the Indian fleet."

The Indian delegation did not find the new British Government totally sensitive to the Indian reasoning of the Chinese submarine threat in the Bay of Bengal. VAdm Hiranandani, in his book 'Transition to Triumph' states, "The British Prime Minister Harold Wilson remarked, half humorously, to Mr Chavan; "I did not know that submarines could climb the Himalayas."

Mr Chavan's 12 – 20$^{th}$ November 1964 visit to Britain was a huge disappointment. On his return, the inevitable happened, and India reopened its negotiations with the Soviet Union.

VAdm B.S. Soman, who was the Chief of the Naval Staff in 1963, writes in the Indian navy magazine Quarter Deck, "A serious bone of contention with the Government was the acquisition of submarines. I was convinced that these were crucial for a balanced force, but Prime Minister Nehru and Admiral Mountbatten thought otherwise."

"After a lot of discussions, I was allowed to raise the matter with the Admiralty when I went to Britain in 1963. As expected, they turned it down - it was clear that the British would only sell us vessels that conformed to their Commonwealth Indian Ocean Defence Plan. This was not acceptable to the Navy, and I recommended that we look elsewhere, suggesting that Russia might be a likely substitute."

"We found the Russians not only were ready to sell but to accept part of the payment in rupees. Thus it came about that the Russians got our custom and remained our major and reliable suppliers over the years."

The Soviets had enthusiastically recommended submarines for the Indian Navy. The then Indian ambassador to the Soviet Union Mr T.N. Kaul recalls in his book 'Stalin to Gorbachev and Beyond' that in 1963 he asked the Russian Defence Minister Marshal Malinovsky the sort of defence preparedness India needed against the Chinese threat. Marshal Malinovsky replied that India needed a strong and mobile Army, Navy, and Air Force, well equipped with the latest weapons. Instead of a prestigious, overhauled, old British aircraft carrier (which he called the fifth leg of a dog and an easy target), India should go in for a submarine fleet to guard her long coastline.

The British and Americans were not the only hurdle for the submarine acquisition. The navy itself was hesitant about switching over to the Soviet Union for its warship needs. VAdm S.N. Kohli (later Adm & CNS), who was the Deputy Chief of the Naval Staff in 1965, writes in his memoirs titled ' We Dared - Maritime Operations in the 1971 Indo Pak War', "Having tried both the USA and UK and drawn a blank from both countries, we had no alternative but to go to the Soviet Union. This decision was taken after the most careful consideration as it would mean going to the Communist camp for the first time. We are often blamed by spokesmen from Western countries, more particularly the USA, for going to Russia - but they are not aware that a first approach to their country had drawn a blank."

In 1964, submarines had finally made it into the 1964-1969 Defence Plan.

Around the same time, the regional Indian Ocean dynamics had changed unfavourably to India's liking. Events related to Pakistan and Indonesia raised concerns among the Indian policymakers. In 1964 the Indonesian and the Pakistan Navies had decided to hold joint exercises, and in 1965 India and Pakistan fought a war that saw limited naval action. While India kept its navy in a defensive position, Pakistan shelled the Indian city of Dwarka, killing a cow.

Pakistan had acquired its first submarine PNS Ghazi (ex USS Diabolo), in 1964 and was fielded against India in 1965. The Indonesians had dispatched two Soviet-made Whiskey class submarines to Pakistan to deter India and also threatened to open another war front in the Andaman and Nicobar islands (as per a book - Story of Pakistan Navy, 1947-72). The submarines reached Pakistan only after the war due to the distance involved.

The Afro–Asian Conference at Bandung in 1955 had seen the deterioration of relations between Indonesia and India due to differing views towards Communist China. The Communist Party of Indonesia government had close links with the Chinese.

Later Indonesia signed a mutual defence arrangement with Pakistan and began claims to the Great Nicobar Island, the Indian territory closest to the Indonesian Sumatra island. The Indonesian's also wanted to rename the Indian Ocean as the Indonesian Ocean. In addition, the Soviets had sold a lot of military hardware to the Indonesians between 1959 and 1965, including fourteen submarines.

The Indian naval planners now had to deal with another potential enemy besides Pakistan and China.

Officially, the Indians underplayed the Indonesian threat and solved the boundary issue.

With submarines entering into the official list of Indian naval purchase plans and the submarine threats from the neighbours, the government sent a defence delegation led by the Defence Production Secretary Mr G. L. Seth to Moscow in 1965 for the acquisition of the Soviet naval armaments. The naval personnel included in the delegations were RAdm S. N. Kohli, Captain B.K. Dang and Lieutenant Commander K. S. Subra-Manian.

The deal to purchase naval equipment from the Soviets was inked on 01$^{st}$ September 1965, which included submarines. Without disclosing the details, the signing of the agreement was formally announced in the Parliament by defence minister Mr Chavan on 06$^{th}$ September (as per Keesing's Contemporary Archives 1965-66, 21036C). The Australian newspaper 'Age' published more details about the deal on 24$^{th}$ November 1965. It stated, "Soviet experts would also help plan a new east coast shipyard at Visakhapatnam, and the deal was reported to include the purchase of four submarines, 'a number' of missile boats, patrol craft and landing craft."

The information flowed in bits and pieces as the Soviets were concerned about information leakages to U.S. and Western countries on the capabilities and limitations of the Soviet equipment being supplied. The navy enforced strict information security at Visakhapatnam, which to a lot of extent remains even now. Recalls an ex-Indian Navy submariner who was among the commissioning team of the third F class submarine "The decision to base the submarines in Visakhapatnam was due to a finger-like projection built into the sea that could restrict the visibility of the ships and submarines in the dockyard. Bombay (now Mumbai) offered ample visibility." Western Naval observers suspected that Visakhapatnam was a Soviet Naval base to support Indian Ocean deployments.

One of the key features of soviet deals was the lack of strings attached to the sale of weapons, unlike the West, which imposed multiple preconditions.

To support the four submarines, the Soviets had agreed to supply India with a submarine depot ship (Amba). Land-based facilities offered included setting up a new Naval Dockyard in Visakhapatnam, which included a Submarine Base, a Submarine Headquarter, and an Integrated Training Establishment.

The Indian Navy began preparations for sending its personnel to the Soviet Union for the induction of the first submarine. Fifteen officers and one hundred and thirty sailors were selected and were given a Russian language course. In Russia, the personnel received training in both theoretical aspects for nine months. Subsequently, they were given training in an F Class submarine.

Adm Kohli states in his book, "The first submarine was to be ready at the end of 1967. The Soviets undertook to train two complete submarine crews in their naval base at Vladivostok on the Pacific Coast. Our crews began their training in July 1966. Credits were made available by the Soviet Union, and the payments were to be made in Rupees. The price of each submarine was around three crores."

It is interesting to note that in the mid-1960s, the Nomenclature Policy was revised, and the submarines were to be named after the various species of fish such as Husa and Matsya.

# FOXTROTS – THE KALVARI CLASS

*The great thing about the Foxtrot was its simplicity of design, based on the reliable Second World War German Type 21 submarines...the Foxtrot did forgive some mistakes, which in other more advanced subs could have been disastrous.*
**VAdm A.K. Singh** (Retd.)

The Foxtrot class is the NATO reporting name for the class of diesel-electric patrol submarines which the Soviets had designated as Project I641. Foxtrots were improved Zulu Class submarines with many features adopted from the highly advanced German Type XXI U-boat. These subs had safety features either in duplicate or in triplicate. They could circumnavigate the earth with a single fuelling and endurance of up to 40 days patrol. The F Class could perform underwater operations continuously for four days, after which they had to rise to a snorkel depth of 7 meters for exchanging air and recharging the batteries. The three diesel engines with three propellers made it noisier than the western counterparts.

The four Soviet F Class submarines arrived between July 1968 and May 1970. These were variants of the early Soviet Foxtrot-class and not suited to Indian tropical conditions.

The first one to arrive was INS Kalvari (Tiger Shark) escorted by INS Talwar (F140), a Type 12, Whitby class anti-submarine frigate. The F class submarines are called the Kalvari class by the Indian Navy. Designated as B-51, the construction of INS Kalvari (S23) began on 27$^{th}$ December 1966 at Novo-Admiralty. The submarine was commissioned under the command of Commander K.S. Subra-Manian on 8th December 1967 in the Soviet Riga Sea Port. As the Suez Canal was closed due to the Arab-Israel conflict, Kalvari sailed about 19,000 miles to reach INS Virbahu, the first Indian Submarine base located in Visakhapatnam. She was berthed at the Base Repair Organisation (BRO) Jetty (now known as Naval Dockyard). A guard was posted at the approach to Kalvari and was barricaded. Indian Navy celebrates the 8th December as Submarine Day to commemorate the induction of its first submarine.

RAdm J.M.S. Sodhi (Retd.), who was among the commissioning crew of Kalvari, writes in Quarterdeck, "There were two major issues to be resolved before we set sail for India. The first was how many officers and sailors from the Soviet Navy would come with us to India as the Soviets stated that for all their previous submarines sold to foreign countries, the full Soviet crew also came on board. Here the Captain of Kalvari noted that there was no requirement of any Soviet crew to come with us to India as he was competent to command the submarine, and the crew was fully trained. Unfortunately, Naval Headquarters felt otherwise and decided that the Soviet Commanding Officer, Engineer Officer and one Communication sailor was to accompany us and regrettably, they were really given the cold shoulder on board.

"The next issue was for a ship to escort us. Here again, the Commanding Officer felt there was no requirement, but INS Talwar, under the command of the then Commander O.S. Dawson, was sent to Riga to escort us. Now the fun and games started. Firstly, we were denied shore accommodation in foreign ports as we had to be accommodated onboard Talwar and I remember having slept on the floor of a cabin occupied by an officer much junior to me. Then Talwar was required to fuel very often, and she visited over 20 ports as against our four and was in fact hardly escorting us but always sailing to fuel.

"Thus, during the 90-day passage, Talwar was with us only for approximately 10-15 days. Fortunately, Naval Headquarters realized its mistake, and thenceforth none of the submarines was escorted except for INS Khandheri, which Submarine Depot Ship INS Amba accompanied after commissioning in Odessa. All the remaining submarines came unescorted, and the crew had proper rest and recreation during their long voyages to India.

"It may be mentioned that the Suez Canal was closed and our submarines had to come via the Cape of Good Hope and cross the equator twice during the passage to India. Very few submariners had the opportunity to sail around the Cape of Good Hope on three occasions and I was one of them together with Commodore P.S. Bawa and Commodore Gilbert Menezes.

"On arrival in Indian waters, we were met by INS Betwa and escorted to Visakhapatnam where the Chief of the Naval Staff, Admiral A.K. Chatterjee was present on the jetty to receive us. On the same day, the foundation stones of the Submarine Base Complex (Virbahu and Satavahana) and the Naval Dockyard Visakhapatnam were laid."

Later, INS Khanderi (S22), INS Karanj (S21) and INS Kursura (S20) joined INS Kalvari to form the first submarine squadron named 8$^{th}$ SM Sqn. Maybe the number 8 had to do with the date of commissioning - 08th December 1967. Commanding Officer of Virbahu was also designated as Captain SM 8. The Kalvari class submarines were inducted under the watch of Admiral and Chief of the Naval Staff Adm A.K. Chatterji. Captain B.K. Dang was the first Director Submarine Arm.

It is interesting to note that Khanderi broke its radio during its voyage from the Soviet Union to India. She was passing through European waters during the time of the incident. Radio silence for 2-3 days raised alarm bells in India. It was the first and probably the last time the navy raised the 'Submiss' (submarine missing, initial search for the submarine) code word. In the meantime, the submarine crew managed to repair their radio and communicate after borrowing a repair kit from a passing civilian ship.

Kursura was commissioned at Soviet Riga port on 18th December 1969 under the command of Commander A. Auditto. She sailed for India on 20th February 1970. During her 31 years of service, the submarine has traversed 73,500 nautical miles participating in almost all types of Naval operations. Kursura played an important role in the 1971 Indo-Pak war. She was the pioneer submarine extending goodwill and harmony through visits and flag-showing missions to other nations. Kursura hosted 13 commanding officers, the last being Cdr. K.M. Sreedharan.

She was laid off for many years to be cannibalised for spare parts for other submarines but underwent a Medium Refit in Naval Dockyard in Visakhapatnam (ND(V)) in 1978 and came out in 1991.

On 24th April 2000, she was successfully beached and hauled up on R..K. Beach, Visakhapatnam, to be a submarine museum. After being beached, Kursura was decommissioned on 27th February 2001. Even though Kursura is now under a municipal body, the navy still goes with the formality of 'Dressing ship' on important days like August 15th, January 26th and December 4th Navy Day.

Khanderi was the first to be decommissioned on 18th October 1989, serving only 21 years.

During their service lives, Kalvari and Kursura were upgraded to the I641M standard. Karanj became the testbed for several DRDO made technologies and systems like the Rani Radar, Panchendriya Sonar and Tactical Weapon Control System. These were installed during the course of refits.

Likewise, Kursura was used for test firing the DRDO's Naval Science & Technological Laboratory Naval Science & Technological Laboratory (NSTL) NST 58 torpedo in 1975. NST 58 was a project to convert Soviet origin 53-56 torpedo into a passive homer.

Foxtrot Class Surfacing - Caricatures like this have kept naval magazines Quarter Deck and Periscope Engrosing

# FOXTROTS – THE VELA CLASS

*The decommissioning of the last of the Vela Class submarine is a poignant moment in the history of the Submarine Arm. These submarines were the platforms on which several generations of submariners learned the art and craft of submarining.*

**VAdm K.N Sushil** (Retd.)

The naval leadership appeared reluctant to purchase additional submarines until the Pakistan Navy received three Daphné-class submarines from France in the 1970s. Based on the navy's recommendation, the Indian government placed an order for additional four submarines of the F-class in 1971. They were to be based on the west coast.

Vela Class or the V Class was the new I641 class called I641K, which had improvements over the F class after Soviet interactions with the Indian Navy. Vela class had better sensors and an improved Fire Control System (FCS). The sonars were of more modern vintage; the Electronic Support Measures (ESM) was also of a modernised version. FCS was modernised but of the same principle.

The Kalvari class had Artika as active and Feniks as passive sonars, while in the Vela class, they were MGK 200 and MG 10M, respectively. Naval submariners have high regard for the sonars on Vela. Since submarines mostly work passive sonars, the submariners say that MG 10M was an excellent sonar and way ahead of its time.

These submarines were suited for Indian tropical conditions based on the experiences operating the

Kalvari class submarines. The key improvements included choosing equipment and machinery for higher ambient temperature, seawater temperature and relative humidity; better active and passive sonar, including long-range passive sonar; and control room layout changes.

INS Vagli - Foxtrot Class

Basic infrastructure for maintenance and repairs was set up at Bombay, and the submarines arrived in Bombay between January 1974 and May 1975. As an interim measure, the submarine depot ship INS

Amba was moved to Bombay to support the Vela class submarines till the facilities were created.

The first of her class, INS Vela, was commissioned into the Indian Navy on 31$^{st}$ August 1973. Vela reached Bombay in January 1974, after stops at Gothenburg in Sweden, La-Havre in France, Las-Palmas in the Canary Islands and an unscheduled stopover at Walvis Bay to drop a sick officer. Vela arrived to lay the foundation of the 9$^{th}$ Submarine Squadron on the Western Seaboard. Vela was the first submarine to be based at Bombay. She was in Vladivostok in September 1980 for medium refit and returned in December 1992. In the same year, she was shifted base port to Visakhapatnam in 1992. Vela was awarded the coveted Unit Citation in 2004-2005. In 2006, Vela was deployed for 45 days, clocking 2378 dived hours in that cycle, the maximum by any Foxtrot to date. She was decommissioned on 25$^{th}$ June 2010.

INS Vela (S40), INS Vagir (S41), INS Vagil (S42) and INS Vagsheer (S43) constituted the 9th squadron. In total, the Foxtrot class submarines served the Navy for 43 years.

# THE SWEDISH OFFER

The Indian Navy has a long-standing objective of indigenous construction of the equipment it uses. From the 1950s, the navy began sending its engineers abroad to learn design in all required disciplines. Having matured and mastered the exploitation and maintenance skills on the I641 submarine's in the 1960s, the navy began looking for construction of the submarines indigenously.

On 7th September 1970, the Times of India quoted Deputy Minister for defence production P.C. Sethi stating in the Parliament that a proposal to manufacture the submarines in India with a foreign collaborator was being actively considered. Jane's International Defence Review dated 4/1974 on Page 530 stated that India was close to signing an agreement with Sweden for indigenous manufacture of the A14 class submarine. It stated that the Swedish offer was being considered after unsuccessful negotiations with the Soviet Union. The details of the deal are now available in a declassified report from the United States, currently posted on the whistleblower website Wikileaks.

The declassified document dated May 1974 quotes a source at the Swedish embassy in New Delhi confirming to the US embassy that the facts of the submarine deal were essential as stated in Indian press reports of May 6 and 7. He denied that the deal had been concluded, and a leak of the story in Stockholm could torpedo it. Below is the verbatim reproduction of the declassified document.

The source agreed with (US) embassy official's surmise that opponents of the deal in the Swedish government had probably leaked the story to wreck it. The source said the deal was discussed during the visit of the Swedish Supreme military commander to India a few months ago. Latter was accompanied by Secretary of State for Defense (Anders) Thunborg.

The source characterized Thunborg as part of "India Mafia" in Sweden, having acquired contacts in India in earlier days of activity in Swedish and International Socialist Youth Affairs. One of Thunborg's old Indian friends is Minister of State for Defence Production V.C. Shukla. According to the source, the Indian's have been buying Soviet Submarines but are dissatisfied with them. Shukla-Thunborg connection gave the Indians the possibility of obtaining superior merchandise from politically acceptable sources. Thunborg was receptive and, following his visit, sent a team from the Swedish State-owned shipbuilding company Kockums in Karlskrona.

The shipbuilding team negotiated a deal involving production in Sweden of initially two "sjee-orm" (Sea Snake) submarines. Sea Snake is described as the advanced version of Näcken Class (A-14). The Indian technicians would participate in construction and would then build more submarines under license in India. The deal also envisioned assistance to the Indian shipbuilding industry, both military and civilian.

In the course of talks, the Indians expressed hope that soft SIDA (Swedish International Development Authority) loans could be used to finance the submarine deal. Request embarrassed the Swedes, whose policy is to allow aid recipients complete freedom in choosing to what purpose aid funds should be put, but who thought aid financing of military purchases would be beyond SIDA's terms of reference. The source implied that SIDA funds had been ruled out of the deal.

The Source concluded his briefing with the comment that leak would deeply embarrass Indians, and Soviets would be displeased to learn of contemplated deal.

Another declassified document dated 7$^{th}$ June 1974 states that India planned to build up to 20 submarines after purchasing two or three submarines constructed in Sweden.

Joseph P. Chacko

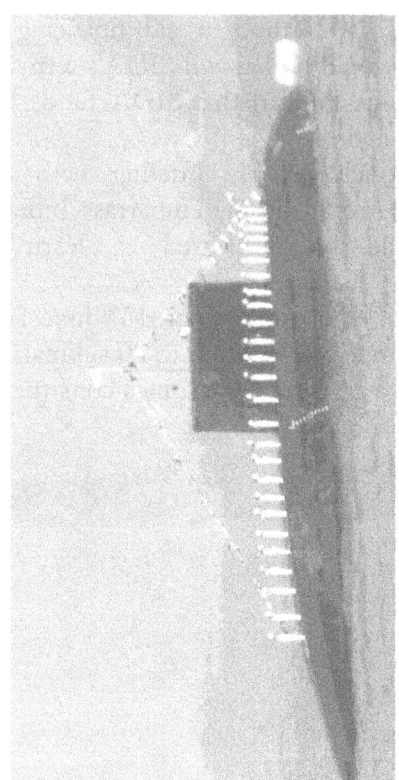

Submarine dressed overall with the Garland on which flags and pennants are dressed for ceremony. The white object on the water level is the bouy to which the sub is moored. Image : Joseph P. Chacko

# HDW TYPE 1500 – SHISHUMAR CLASS

*Building a submarine is a very complex business. It is one of the most complex and sophisticated design and manufacturing operations imaginable – it really is. It's not all that different from building a space probe, it really is that difficult and that sophisticated.*
**Tony Abbott**, Australian Prime Minister

Since the Foxtrots were suited for deepwater requirements, the navy felt a need for acquiring submarines suited for the shallow water uses and began discussing the possibility of acquiring a Sub Surface killer (SSK) design by Professor Ulrich Gabler. VAdm Mihir K. Roy writes in his book 'War in the Indian Ocean "at this juncture, Naval Headquarters was negotiating with the well-known German designer, Professor Gabler, for an ocean-going submarine to be jointly constructed in Italy/India as submarine construction was prohibited in Germany. However, British intelligence got wind of these negotiations and instead signed an agreement with Professor Gabler possibly to thwart India's aim to initiate an indigenous submarine programme."

After failing to buy submarines from the British and the Swedes in the 1960s, this was for the third time that India was attempting to buy submarines from Western sources. VAdm Hiranandani explains the rationale for the selection of a western design in the book 'Transition to Eminence', "In 1975, the Apex Defence Review Committee supported the navy's proposal for constructing submarines. The Soviet Union had already indicated that it did not have submarines of the size that the Navy was looking for. In 1977, the Government accepted the requirement for looking at alternate sources for building submarines."

After the government nod, a four-man naval delegation headed by RAdm N.P. Dutta arrived in Europe for evaluation of the European submarine building yards in May 1977. The team visited shipbuilders Direction Techniques des Construction Navales (DTCN) - France, Kockums - Sweden, Howaldtswerke Deutsche Werft AG (HDW) - Germany, Thyssen Nordseewerke GmbH (TNSW) - Germany and designers Nevesbu B.V. - Holland.

During the visit, DTCN gave reluctant access to an Agosta in construction. In Holland, Nevesbu displayed two designs, but they were too small for the requirement. Kockums offered a conceptual Type 471 design which was their first effort at developing an export submarine. HDW was the only submarine yard that had the expertise of constructing submarines that operated pre and post-World War II.

Tenders were issued after the naval team conducted the evaluations. Following submarines were offered for the tender:

HDW 209 class
TNSW Thyssen 1500/1700
Italcantieri Sauro class (Italy)
DTCN Super Agosta
Kockums Type 471
Nevesbu Zwaardvis (Sword Fish)

The British did not offer a submarine, while Holland and France withdrew from the tender after the navy asked the shipyards for the willingness to modify their submarine designs to suit the qualitative requirements.

In February 1979, the Cabinet Committee on Political Affairs (CCPA), headed by the then Prime Minister Morarji Desai, approved SSK's for the Navy with a diving depth of 350 metres. The navy would acquire the technology through a transfer and begin co-production of four submarines in India at an estimated cost of Rs.350 crore.

**INS Shalki at MDL before launch**

The same month a nine-member negotiating committee headed by additional secretary of defence M.K. Mukherjee shortlisted Kockums, Italcantieri, HDW and TNSW for further processes. A Policy Technical Delegation visited Sweden, Germany and Italy in May 1979 to allay the fears of their technology falling into the Soviet hands due to Indian proximity with the Soviet Union. Germany also had the policy to discourage arms sales to potential conflict zones. The Policy Technical Delegation assured the European Shipbuilders on the safety of their technology, and the clause was to be built into an Inter-Government Memorandum of Understanding (MOU).

On 16th May, a six-member expert committee

headed by RAdm S.L. Sethi, including Director Submarine Arm (DSA) Captain M. Kondath, submitted its report to the Vice Chief of Naval Staff, giving preference to the Kockums offer followed by the Italcantieri offer. The HDW offer was rejected as it could dive to the depth of only 250 metres. By June 15$^{th,}$ the committee added HDW back on its list with a clause that it can be considered if the diving depth could be improved. In the same month, a delegation led by RAdm D.S. Paintal, including Captain Kondath and ministers from various departments, surveyed various shipyards in Europe and concluded that the Kockums offer was the best.

Meanwhile, the government led by Mrs Indira Gandhi assumed power which led to a change in the composition of the CCPA. The defence Ministry submitted a draft paper for the CCPA listing Kockums as the best deal against the more expensive HDW. The CCPA then approved the shortlisting of both Kockums and HDW on 10$^{th}$ April 1980. A reconstituted committee including VAdm N.R. Dutta, Chief of the Mazagon Docks LTD (MDL), toured Germany and Sweden in May and on 17$^{th}$ May, the committee switched the preference from Kockums to HDW as the Kockums cost had gone up. On 30$^{th}$ June 1980, the CCPA met and approved the HDW deal.

The Agreement on Technical Assistance between the German and Indian Ministry of Defence was signed in July 1981. It was followed up with contracts on 11$^{th}$ December 1981.

The contract stipulated the construction of four submarines with an option for two more at a later stage. The supply of wire-guided torpedoes from

Germany was a part of the deal. Two submarines were to be constructed at the HDW yard in Germany, along with training of the Indian personnel on the project. Two submarines were to be built in India via the transfer of technology and material packages. The optional two packages were to be ordered before December 1982 at baseline cost. The navy selected the Type 209/1500 designed by Ingenieur Kontor Lübeck (IKL), headed by Prof. Ulrich Gabler and asked for an integrated escape sphere in the design. The sphere is located at the forward end of the sail and accommodates 40 crew with air supply up to 8 hours. The Type 1500 built for India was the first of larger sized submarines of the 209 Class.

The first submarine INS Shishumar (S44), was commissioned in 1986 under the command of Commander P. M. Bhate. The submarine class was also named Shishumar. INS Shankush (S45) was commissioned on 20$^{th}$ November 1986.

There was considerable delay in the indigenously constructed submarines as the Indian shipyard MDL faced technological issues, including quality welding arising out of preheating. The German technicians rejected the weld, and the hull had to be dismantled and welded again. The first MDL built submarine INS Shalki (S46), was commissioned on 7$^{th}$ February 1992. The second Submarine INS Shankul (S47) was commissioned on 28$^{th}$ May 1994 by Prime Minister P.V. Narasimha Rao.

Contrary to popular perception, Shalki was not assembled from Completely Knocked Down (CKD) kits. The construction of the submarine at MDL involved similar work as carried out at HDW, and the material package was of the same form as the ones used by foreign yards. The pressure hull and the non-pressure hull structures were rolled, shaped and fabricated in MDL from raw plates and sections supplied by HDW. The equipment manufactured by MDL were hydraulic power packs, drive gears for hydroplanes, rudders and capstan hull valves, torpedo flaps and guide rails, pressure-tight bulkheads and their operating mechanisms and a host of fittings.

Due to the delay in indigenous construction schedules, the option to acquire two more material packages could not be exercised by 1982. Even though the HDW had assured to hold the price, the negotiations could begin only by October 1985 and by then price of the material packages had shot up by approximately 70%. The navy also wanted improvements in the two packages, including a newer MTU engine and torpedoes with fibreglass propeller. The improvement proposal was dropped due to the high costs of the new package and issues with warranties due to delay in construction by MDL. In addition, the 1987 drought led to a change in the financial priorities of the government. There was also a political backlash after the Indian Ambassador to Germany reported a discrepancy in the contractual process, including payment of commissions.

The navy finally discontinued the procurement plan as India was already in talks with the Soviet Union for two additional 877EKM (Kilo Class) submarines, and the navy had six submarines (4 HDW +2 Kilos) it wanted.

The four Shishumar class submarines subsequently underwent midlife upgrades. In the medium refit planned for the Shishumar class during the period 1998-2001, four main systems were to be modernised apart from the other minor ones. These were the main Sonar, Fire Control System, ESM System and the Periscope. The Main Sonar fitted from commissioning was CSU34 from Germany. This was to be upgraded to CSU 90, which permitted low-frequency operations and analysis with a Flank Array. The other equipment was of U.S origin and had been in principal agreed with them for upgradation in the work package.

India conducted a series of nuclear tests in May 1998, inviting sanctions from the U.S, Germany and some other countries. Therefore the ESM, FCS and the Periscopes were not changed in Shishumar. Some other things like the plotting table, the Inertial Navigation Gyro were changed. Thus the work package for the modernisation in the medium refit was curtailed. This issue was addressed in the work package for the second boat Shankush for which the work package and modernisation was very extensive. The FCS Combat System, the Sonar was the same as CSU 90 under the option clause. Among periscopes, one with a non-hull penetrating mast with a laser range finding capability gave more space in the control room. The FCS tender was won by ATLAS Elektronik for the ISUS-90 combat management system and the periscopes were won by Carl Zeiss. The ESM was DR 3000 from France. The submarine-fired torpedo decoy dispensers and a self-noise monitoring system is C-310 from Alenia Sistemi Subacquei. A whole lot of other electronics systems were also changed.

In each contract, there was an inbuilt option clause that was to cater for retro fitment on Shishumar class in its next current refit. Subsequently, there was standardised equipment fit for the next two submarines, Shalki and Shankush. The standardisation came after a protracted battle with the Ministry of Defence (Finance) (MOD (Fin)), who wanted the navy to go for competitive bidding for each. The navy took the stand that there was no guarantee that the same vendor as Shankush would win, and the navy could not afford to have different equipment on four submarines of the same class. It would also be a nightmare for training, documentation and repairs. Ultimately after a two year battle with the MOD (Fin), the navy prevailed. The navy, based on their experience of Shishumar and Shankush, insisted that the medium refit and modernisation should be only with MDL to ensure single-point accountability. The contracts for the nominated equipment by Naval Head Quarters (NHQ) for the modernisation should be contracted by MDL. This was also resisted by the MOD (Fin), but the navy prevailed in the end. This was for the first time that the procurement of the equipment was offloaded to the yard. Cmde Arun Kumar was the Principal Director Submarine Acquisition (PDSMAQ) for planning Medium Refit cum Modernisation for 2nd, 3rd and 4th SSKs. The actual refit for 3rd and 4th boats commenced in 2006 and 2008 after he retired.

To keep up with the updates, the Attack Simulator at INS Vajrabahu, Mumbai base, was also upgraded to a reference system that replicates the complete dry end of the sonar cum Fire control system installed on-board to carry out realistic training for the submarine crew.

Shishumar class submarines are armed with the German ATLAS ELEKTRONIK made 20km range

SUT-66 Mod-1 wire-guided torpedo. The navy has already entered into a contract with the company to upgrade them. The upgrade is expected to extend the life of the torpedoes by at least 15-17 years.

The navy is now looking for a Service Life Extension Program (SLEP) for the Shishumar class. On 9th February 2014, Shepherd Media quoted a ThyssenKrupp Marine Systems spokesman stating that its submarine making arm HDW had received an RFP (Request for proposal) for the Shishumar upgrade at the end of 2013 and would be responding to the proposal by March 2014. The spokesman said that the navy wants to bring in new systems. He said the facilities in Germany would have to be prepared, and the company will install the new kit at the Indian Navy's shipyard in Mumbai for future repairs and maintenance. The spokesman said that two boats out of the four are expected to be upgraded with UGM-84L Harpoon Block II Encapsulated Missiles.

The Harpoon capability is likely to be introduced in Shalki and Shankul, the last two submarines constructed in the series. The first two submarines are already reaching the end of their 30-year operational life and are not expected to be upgraded.

The inclusion of Air Independent Propulsion (AIP) is also a possibility for the last two submarines of the Shishumar class. On 06th September 2004, United News of India (UNI) reported that Germany-based Siemens had offered to upgrade the Shishumar Class submarines, including installing an AIP system. Siemens has developed the PEM (Polymer Electrolyte Membrane) fuel cell modules which generate energy by converting hydrogen and oxygen into electricity.

However, a DRDO lab 'Naval Materials Research

laboratory' (NMRL), has also created an AIP system based on fuel cell technology. The author had seen the concept prototype during a visit to NMRL in 2008. On 19th April 2011, the author owned publication Frontier India stated that the DRDO had successfully developed the AIP prototype and began creating a land-based AIP system for demonstration purposes. One of the key differentiators of DRDO AIP is the zero discharge of fuel into the water, resulting in a decrease in the infra-red signature. The discharge can be collected in bottles and disposed of once it arrives at the base.

**Sishumar Class submarine on a pontoon**

# 877EKM - THE KILO - SINDHUGHOSH CLASS

*"Black Holes."*
**US Navy**

Kilo is the NATO reporting name of the Soviet-era naval diesel-electric submarine, which is designated as Project 877 Varshavyanka. The later version, Project 636, has been dubbed as 'black hole' by the U.S. Navy for its level of quietness.

In 1983, the navy evaluated the Type 877EKM submarines on an invitation by the Soviet Ambassador in Delhi. At the time, the two countries were negotiating the lease of a nuclear submarine to India. The navy found the Kilo hunter-killer SSK comparable to the HDW - 1500 approved to be built in India and could operate in relatively shallow waters. In view of the decreasing force levels due to the problems of the mid-life refit of the Foxtrot submarines, the navy decided to acquire eight Type 877EKM submarines.

The contract for procurement of the first six submarines was inked in 1984. 1987 and 1988 saw the contracts for the seventh and eighth submarines, respectively. The deliveries were completed between 1986 -1990, and two more squadrons were established.

The contracts for the final two submarines, the 9$^{th}$ and the 10$^{th,}$ were signed on 30$^{th}$ November 1997. The 9$^{th}$ was delivered in 3 months, and the 10$^{th}$ was handed over on 20$^{th}$ July 2000. In 1994, the Russians had offered the Tube Launched Missile capability for the 877EKM's. The 10th submarine had the TLM capability. Later all Kilo's except Sindhudhvaj and Sindhuvir received the TLM capability. All kilos with TLM anti-ship capability were also upgraded with Land attack TLM during the medium refits.

The names of the submarines in the series are Sindhughosh (S55), Sindhudhvaj (S56), Sindhuraj (S57), Sindhuvir (S58), Sindhuratna (S59), Sindhukesari (S60), Sindhukirti (S61), Sindhuvijay (S62), Sindhurakshak (S63) and Sindhushastra (S65).

By the end of the decade, India had a formidable force of five submarine squadrons.

The Kilo-class submarines have a displacement of 2,300 tons, length of 72.6 meters, the surface speed of 10 knots, a submerged speed of 19 knots (about 35 km/hr), test depth (maximum depth at which a submarine is permitted to dive) of 300 meters, the operational range of 6,000 miles (over 9500 km's), an endurance of 45 days and a crew of 52. Armament includes six 533-mm torpedo tubes.

The Soviets had made great advances in submarine sonars. The MGK 400 sonar fitted on the Kilo-class were also fitted on the INS Chakra (Charlie-I Class nuclear submarine). Indian submariners found the MGK 400 as an outstanding sonar, far superior to its contemporaries like CSU 34, which was of similar vintage on the Shishumar class.

In the course of modernisation, the submarines are equipped with an advanced Russian Club-S cruise missile system (developed by Novator Design Bureau) with a firing range of about 200 km, Indian sonar USHUS and radio communication systems CCS-MK.

A second round of upgrades for Kilo Submarines may be on cards. On 22nd August 2013, the Russian news agency RIA reported a visit by an Indian military delegation to St. Petersburg to discuss military-technical collaboration in submarine-building. It quoted a Russian defense industry source stating that the talks with the Indian delegation headed by the Indian Navy's Chief of Material, VAdm Nadella Niranjan Kumar, included the possibility of a second round of upgrading for India's Kilo-class (Project 877EKM) diesel-electric submarines.

On 14$^{th}$ August 2013, the Sindhurakshak sank after explosions on board when the submarine was berthed at Mumbai. The Indian media has speculated on the lease of an additional Kilo-class submarine from Russia to offset the loss of Sindhurakshak and maintain the combat readiness of its submarine fleet.

## The air conditioning and other issues

The Kilo-class in the Indian naval service has suffered a number of issues, and the navy has tried to solve them with ingenious and indigenous efforts. The primary issue has been the air conditioning. The Russian design Bureau was aware of the air-conditioning requirement for tropical conditions but could not meet it.

The air conditioning issue exists due to two factors. First, the AC capacity of 55000 Kcal/hour is inadequate in tropical conditions. Secondly, the airflow inside was not efficient, which further reduced the efficiency of the AC.

The navy resorted to ingenious measures like replacing normal incandescent lights with tubes to reduce emitted heat to solve the issue. Subsequently, a split ac was installed in the control room. Later, a firm in Chennai installed an indigenised AC with a capacity of nearly 100000 Kcal/hour. But there was very little difference and also led to imbalances in the load calculations on the main batteries. In 2003, the navy ordered the in house Department Of Naval Design (Submarine Design Group) (DND (SDG)) to conduct a comprehensive air flow study and then come up with a proper AC requirement. It is believed that the problem has been solved.

There were many other changes that were undertaken in the Kilo-class submarines. The water distiller on board which was a sedimentation type, was changed with RO plant from Rochem. The distilled water capacity was inadequate, and it was solved by carrying extra Syntex made tanks. The electrical compressors were replaced by indigenous ones from Sulzer India. The carbon brushes of the commutators of the main Generators were changed with those from Assam Carbons as the original Russian ones would spark at more than 2/3 loads in Indian ambient conditions.

The HP air and Hydraulic pipelines had pitting leading to pinholes on the lead boat Sindhughosh and were replaced with ones supplied by Midhani.

The original paint in the battery pits was not good enough to withstand the hostile acidic conditions that lead to the pressure hull pitting. This was a very serious issue so the Navy used the paint V61, which was employed in the Shishumar class as also formulating Standard Operating Procedures (SOP) for washing down the pits with distilled water (DW) in the harbour and reducing the requirement of the overall measurement of cells to be done only in harbour to prevent spillage of electrolyte if done at sea.

The naval personnel had an extensive discussion with the submarine designer, Mr. Yuri Kormilitsin on all these issues. All this led to the Russians modifying the design leading to improved Kilos named as Type 636.

## Was the Kilo design originally intended for nuclear propulsion?

In his book 'Transition to Guardianship', Vice Adm. G.M. Hiranandani writes, "officers who underwent EKM training in Russia had gathered an impression that the submarines' teardrop hull, with sonar waves absorbing anechoic rubber tiles and other features, were meant to be for a nuclear-powered submarine. Because of the technical problems, the reactor could not be integrated, and the submarine design was reverted to conventionally powered."

But it was not true, say the ex-submariners. The Kilo was never designed to have a nuclear reactor. The teardrop hull gives a more efficient hydrodynamic profile resulting in better-submerged control and reduced noise signatures.

INS Sindhuratna arrives in Bombay

# THE INDIAN SUBMARINE DESIGN

*The Indian Navy would be 'truly and totally Indian.'*
**Adm Sushil Kumar** (Retd)


In 1992 the Indian Navy scripted the Staff Requirements for an indigenously made submarine design designated Project 75 (P 75). As Prime Minister Mr. P.V. Narasimha Rao backed the submarine building plan, HDW was not banned, and Mazagon Docks Ltd (MDL) was already experienced in building the Shishumar class submarines, the navy began to explore the construction of two submarines based on the HDW 209/1500 design for quicker turnaround. The HDW Type 1500 model is of 1970's vintage, and the P 75 submarines were required to be less noisy and have the capability of launching Tube Launched Missiles (TLM). A Submarine Design group – DND (SDG) was constituted in Naval Headquarters consisting of personnel who had studied noise reduction for HDW Type 1500 from Germany. A Letter of Intent (LoI) was dispatched to MDL proposing four firms – Thomson CSF (France) (TCSF), Vickers Shipbuilding and Engineering Ltd (UK) (VSEL), Kockums (Sweden) and Rosvoorouzhenie (Russia), for validation of the design and consultancy.

As per the tenth report of Public Accounts Committee (2010) (Ministry of Defence), MDL had tendered inquiries to these four firms, yet a response was received only from TCSF, which was willing to participate in the project on the condition that their Combat Suite was selected for the Submarines. Post due consideration, it was decided to proceed with negotiations with TCSF on the price regarding options offered by them. Accordingly, price negotiations for the construction of two submarines under project P-75 were held between TCSF and MDL from February to June 1999.

Naval authorities who had handled the project confirmed to the author that it was the Navy that had asked for Tube Launched Missile (TLM) Exocet SM39 along-with the TCSF's combat management suite. They reasoned that the submarine of project P-75, which were likely to remain operational for the next 25 to 30 years, must have the capability to launch missiles against enemy targets from underwater. As the supply of Exocet SM39 required French government permission, TCSF agreed to recommend the sale of the missiles to India. The French Government was initially hesitant to permit the sale as it did not agree with the prospect of their missile being integrated with a German submarine.

One of the reasons for the delay in obtaining the approval of CCS for the negotiated price for the 5th & 6th boats was the non-assurance by the French Government for the release of Exocet. Several letters were exchanged on the subject without results. The issue was resolved in May 2000 during a High-level meeting on Indo-French Strategic dialogue between the two Defence Ministers, Mr. Alain Richard and Mr. George Fernandes. The French gave the go-ahead for the Exocet if India took 4 Scorpenes or 2+2 (Scorpene and HDW SSKs). The choice was left to India. Meanwhile, the 30-year submarine building plan had been formulated in 1999, and the French were unaware that the navy was looking at six submarines under P-75.

The project suffered the final blow when the Indian Naval team realized that the scope of HDW involvement was far more than they had imagined. TCSF agreed to manage the HDW liasioning, and the naval project team added that cost under the project management head. The Finance Ministry objected to the sum, which appeared unexplainable.

Mr. Fernandes asked the navy to do a cost-benefit analysis between the two options given by the French. The NHQ concluded that it was better to go for all six Scorpenes as they were contemporary. It would be easier to fit Exocet on Scorpene's French design than on a German hull. Accordingly, CCS was approached in early 2001 to cancel its earlier approval to procure 5th & 6th HDW SSKs and accord a new authorisation to negotiate with TCSF (later Armaris) for 6 Scorpenes on a single Vendor basis. The CCS approved the same in April 2001.

Joseph P. Chacko

# 30 YEAR PLAN FOR SUBMARINE CONSTRUCTION

*There are two clear paths. Do we outsource the design, development, build and maintenance of our submarines - and in doing so, surrender our sovereign independence and gift an entire industry to another country? Or, do we back ourselves and commit to long-term investment in building a robust indigenous capability to deliver and sustain our Navy's future submarines in perpetuity?*
**General Peter Cosgrove**, Chairman, Defence SA Advisory Board (Australia)

The Indian naval planners exhibit little trust in western military suppliers and a bit more in the Russians. The need to complete a self-sufficient indigenous defence-industrial base has always been a high priority for the Indian naval planners. The navy has been trying to indigenise submarine production since the 1970s. The discussions with Sweden and the later HDW deal for Shishumar class were the initial steps towards achieving indigenous submarine production.

After completing two Shishumar class submarines at the Indian yard, the submarine building skills were lost due to a lack of follow on orders. Matters were complicated when the Indian design based on HDW 1500 submarine was dropped due to obsolesce, and DND (SDG) found itself lacking design skills without external consultancy and verification. For the navy, it became necessary to re-learn the submarine construction techniques and submarine design for implementing an indigenous design and manufacture of the submarines in the future. Keeping in view of the shortcomings, the navy embarked on a two-pronged strategy to 'build' and then 'design – build' the submarines in India.

A programme for constructing 24 indigenous conventional submarines, commonly known as the 30-year Plan for submarine construction, was approved by the Cabinet Committee on Security (CCS) of the Government of India in July 1999. The force level of 24 submarines was first derived in the force level plans paper presented in the mid-sixties under the aegis of VAdm A.K. Chatterjee. The number was kept the same in the 30-year plan paper approved by the CCS.

---

The objective of the 30 Year Plan is to create the indigenous capability of a series of construction of submarines in concert with Indian Industry (Public & Private) under the aegis of the Department of Defence Production and the Indian Navy. The Plan is in two phases.

**Phase I:** 1999-2015, in which 12 submarines (6 each under P75 and P75 (I)) are to be built. The former is of a western design such as Type 209 or derivative thereof and under P75 (I) of an Eastern design (Russian) such as 877EKM or Derivative thereof as Type Amur 1650.

**Phase II:** 2015-2030 in which 12 submarines of an indigenous design. It was hoped that this design would incorporate the best features of both the designs used in Phase I.

---

VAdm Chatterjee had planned to base twelve submarines each at the east and west coast of India.

He reasoned that 18 subs would be available for use at any given time, while six go under repairs or refits.

As mentioned in the previous chapter, there was only project P-75 which was the 5th & 6th boats of the Shishumar Class, which was revived in 1993. The government of India issued a Letter of intent (LoI) for building the Type 75 submarine to Mazagon Dock Ltd in 1997. After 1999, it became part of the 30-year plan. The plan was to be implemented in two phases and three stages. In the first stage, six Scorpene submarines were selected for the P-75 project. The Russian Amur 1650 was considered for the P-75 (India) (P-75(I)) project in the second stage, but the Qualitative Requirements were changed in 2006. In Phase II and the 3rd stage targeted for 2015-30, 12 boats of an indigenous design were envisaged to be constructed. As per the original plan, integration with the BrahMos missile is not part of project P-75(I), as it would mean delays. It was to be considered in Phase II.

VAdm Arun Kumar Singh (Retd) is credited with authoring the Indian Navy's 30-year submarine construction program when he was Assistant Chief of Naval Staff (Submarines). Cmde U.N. Chitnavis was the Principal Director of Submarine Acquisition (PDSMAQ) at the time. After CCS approval, the project was steered by Cmde Arun Kumar, who had taken over as PDSMAQ in May 1999.

# PROJECT 75 - THE SCORPENE

*Failure is only the opportunity to begin again, this time more intelligently.*

**Henry Ford**

In November 2001, after the approval from the Indian government, negotiations formally began with TCSF (later Thales) and Armaris on their offer for construction of Scorpene submarines at MDL under project P-75. The first round of the Price Negotiation Committee (PNC) meeting was held from November 2001 to June 2002. After vetting by the Finance Ministry and Central Vigilance Commission, the Contract Negotiating Committee (CNC) held the second meeting in February 2005 and the third one in August 2005. At the same time, HDW offered its U-214 submarines. But since the Delhi High Court had not accepted the closure report on the HDW bribe case, the offer could not be pursued.

In 2002, the Government of India negotiated a contract with MDL for MDL Procured Materials (MPM). The MPM had a budgetary figure of approximately USD 500 million in the MDL contract as per the recommendation of the French-based on economic conditions in July 2000. In the contract, MDL was allowed to procure the same at actuals since in 2002, when the contract with MDL had been negotiated, the main contract for collaboration had not been inked. It was likely that when MDL would finally order the MPM, the prices would have increased. The contract was negotiated for a year and finalised before the commercial negotiations began. Another reason to create MPM was the Indian desire to indigenise the equipment from the 3rd submarine onwards to reach an indigenous content of 65% by the 6th submarine.

The evaluation of the Scorpene submarine was questioned by the Comptroller and Auditor General (CAG) much later, and a report was brought out in 2010, which helps us understand the evaluation process followed during the time. The CAG stated that the Ministry accepted the unproven design of the Scorpene Submarine based on the validation of the design through computer simulation even though the design of the Scorpene Submarine had not proved its efficacy in other navies. In such a scenario, deviations in respect of the prescribed parameters such as stability, speed, endurance, noise levels, manoeuvring performances etc., of the Submarine could not be ruled out.

The MoD, in its reply, stated that as per the Defence Procurement Procedure 2002, a Submarine should be trial evaluated in Indian waters or its design should be validated through Computer simulations and model testing before accepting the proposal for the Submarine. Such evaluations were intended to gauge the Submarine's performance with reference to the Naval Staff Qualitative Requirement (NSQR). The Scorpene design incorporated incremental improvements and underwent state-of-the-art validations by the French. The Ministry stated that Scorpene Submarines have already been commissioned by the Chilean and the Royal Malaysian navies. A delegation of the Indian Navy and Joint Delegation of the Indian Navy and MDL visited France and Spain and even sailed-on-board Chilean Scorpene in Chilean waters besides visiting

Malaysian Scorpene at Kochi at different times to conduct physical verification of the Scorpene Submarines in order to satisfy themselves with the Sea Acceptance Trial (SAT) and Harbour Acceptance Trial (HAT). The MoD did accept the CAG observations and stated that it had inserted specific provisions in the contract regarding corrective actions if the main performance parameters were not met.

Naval officials closely involved with the initial deal say that there is a provision for rejecting the submarine if it does not meet the required parameters. If the required parameters have not been met, the government will decide whether to accept it or not. There are also provisions for a penalty in the case of delay in the project and not meeting the parameters.

In October 2005, the Indian Navy ordered six Scorpene SSKs for Rs. 12022 Crores, with an option for acquiring four more submarines of the class in future. An order for 36 MBDA SM-39 Exocet anti-ship missiles was also placed to arm the submarines. Italy based Whitehead Sistemi Subacquei (WASS) offered it's Black Shark advanced, long-range, multi-purpose, heavy weight torpedo for the project, but a contract was not signed.

For the P-75 project, there were two contracts – one with the Armaris as 'prime collaborator' and the other with MDL as the 'prime contractor. The submarines were to be built under a technology transfer from Armaris, a joint company set up in 2002 by Direction des Constructions Navales (DCN) and THALES. Armaris worked closely with Spain's Navantia (ex Bazan, ex Izar), which co-developed the Scorpene submarine with DCN.

Since this project has the objective to acquire the

industrial know-how to build these submarines in MDL, Armaris had offered an extensive technology transfer (ToT) programme, with technical assistance and equipment provided on the spot. The TOT comprised two parts, the Technical Design Documentation (TDD) and Technical Documentation Production (TDP). MDL had further signed three contracts with Armaris for Manufacturing/ Procurement and delivery of selected submarine equipment's/ items commonly known as MPM to be fitted in the Scorpene submarines.

Navantia was a part of a consortium for the Indian Scorpene deal. Navantia's scope of work in the deal is mentioned on their website. It included:

• A design documentation package enabling MDL in Mumbai and the Indian Navy to implement design changes.

• A constructive documentation package, enabling MDL to build the six submarines at their facilities.

• Technical purchasing specifications enabling MDL to purchase the materials required to build the submarines.

• A logistics information package enabling the Indian Navy to maintain submarines during their service life.

• The manufacturing of a series of materials.

• A set of services linked to the scope of supply, supporting the technology transfer process, namely:

• Industrial audit for the modernization and adaptation of shipyard facilities.

• Industrial training in different techniques (structures, propulsion, electricity, batteries, pipes, painting, accommodation) (other courses part of the scope of supply of DCNS).

- On-site training.
- Construction assistance by means of a permanent team deployed at the shipyard.
- On-call support.
- Supply an information system for the management at MDL of the disclosed technical information (part of DCNS scope of supply).
- Supply of design software licenses (this is part of the DCNS scope of supply).
- Support MDL's purchasing management process with European suppliers.

In 2007, DCN acquired the entire Thales French Naval business and was renamed DCNS. Thales acquired a 25 per cent stake in DCNS. DCNS has assumed the responsibility of all future dealings with India for the project. Thales is the prime contractor for submarine systems.

In December 2006, MDL performed the first steel cut for the first submarine. In the same year, an Indian magazine broke a story on Naval War-Room leak and mentioned the leaking of documents and commission payment in the Scorpene deal. However, the officials close to the deal say that the case had nothing to do with the Scorpene deal. The leak was of Commercial Proposals concerning other projects, but in the drives seized, there was a copy of a presentation made to the Principal Staff Officers in the War Room on the final technical configuration of Scorpene as negotiated. The negotiations had already been completed by that time.

In 2007, the public prosecutor's office in Paris dropped an investigation into Thales for alleged bribery in connection with the Indian contract. A preliminary inquiry was launched in 2004 by the public prosecutor's office in France while probing into Malaysia's purchase of two Scorpenes. The police had also seized documents relating to the Indian Scorpene deal. The public prosecutor's office had taken a number of statements, but the allegation was not established. This case was different from the War-Room leak case.

The same year, it was realized that the MPM cost had gone up to approximately USD 700 million. Despite having a mandate for buying at actuals, MDL decided to ask for a CCS approval. By the time CCS gave approval in March 2010, the price had shot up further to slightly over USD 900 million.

In November 2007, the Indian MoD stated that construction of the six Scorpene submarines at MDL slated for delivery between 2012-2017 was expected to be completed as per schedule.

DCNS opened DCNS India, a 100% subsidiary in March 2009 in Mumbai for technical support of local naval shipyards and industries, developing services using Indian skills, and sourcing for national and international needs.

In January 2011, Mr. Patrick Boissier, Chairman and CEO of DCNS, told a publication 'India Strategic' that MDL had already "absorbed the demanding technologies associated with hull fabrication" and that hulls for the first two submarines had been completed. He said that construction of hulls for the third and fourth submarines was in progress while the frame to receive the hull of the fifth submarine was under manufacture. Speaking about delays in the project, Mr. Patrick said that DCNS was "conducting genuine transfers of technologies and of know-how at an unprecedented level…We are providing our Indian partners with technical assistance to manufacture equipment through indigenisation programmes."

In the same year, DCNS announced two separate indigenisation contracts with India based Flash Force and SEC. "We are in India to establish partnerships with the Indian industry to develop local capability and to perform genuine transfers of technologies. We are providing our Indian partners with know-how and technical assistance to manufacture equipment which will be installed on-board the Scorpene submarines. MDL, our main contractor, is also to sub-contract work to these local players. Together, we are qualifying the suitable companies which are meeting the rigorous specifications needed for the submarines" explained Mr. Bernard Buisson, Managing Director of DCNS India. "The indigenous elements to be installed on-board the P-75 Scorpene submarines represent thousands of articles. These are the equipment, systems and subsystems that are fitted on-board like engines, pumps, valves, accommodation elements, AC and safety equipment, but also the combat and ship control systems. They are part of the MPM, contracted in 2010,' he added (7$^{th}$ June 2011, Frontier India).

It was announced in May 2011 that two Indian naval crews would leave for France for training to operate the Scorpene submarines. Each submarine has only a 36-member crew due to high automation levels.

In August 2012, the DCNS announced the completion of operational and intermediate level crew training sessions of Platform Management System and Steering Console for the Indian Navy. The training was conducted during five weeks at HBL, Hyderabad, for the crew of 1st & 2nd Scorpene submarines and MDL employees, for 45 people. These trainings were initially scheduled in France, but after successful local production, it was decided by DCNS and MDL with the Indian Navy to move a step ahead and conduct these training in India. The Platform Management System (PMS) enables controlling and monitoring the submarine's main installations in propulsion, electricity, safety, auxiliary and stability domains. The steering system controls the motion of the submarine by controlling the hydroplanes and rudder. It also controls the propulsion, regulation and trim systems on board by an interface with PMS. The training comprised of operation and troubleshooting (on-board maintenance) activities as well as of simulation for real-time situations.

Asian Age, dated 31st December 2014, reported the beginning of tests by the first submarine within the yard. According to an official privy to the development, the vessel has finished all "outfitting" of the protruding masts, antennae and the periscope within the conning tower and is undergoing checks for validating their functionality. "The piping, wiring and cabling work inside the boat is also done. We will now test all these by simulating underwater conditions where gases and liquids will be pumped through the pipes to see how everything is performing. The team handling the testing bit is working in full swing on this submarine while another team concerned with the internal work is engaged in the wiring and piping works on the other boats," said the officer.

MDL has given its new schedule for the delivery

of the submarines. The First Scorpene submarine is now scheduled to join the Indian Navy in 2016. Deliveries of the remaining five subs will be completed by 2021.

Mr. Bernard Buisson, MD, DCNS India, was quoted in the September 2014 edition of Force Magazine stating that DCNS India was assisting DRDO in integrating DRDO AIP solution on board the Scorpene Project. "We believe this is a definite possibility for the 5th and 6th submarine without much alteration of the timelines for these submarines," he said. In the December 2014 edition of Geopolitics Magazine, he said that the AIP can be integrated into existing submarines during a future overhaul.

The Indian Navy has not yet finalized the torpedoes for the Scorpene submarines due to allegations of corruption. In 2011, through selection by a global tender, WASS of Italy was selected to supply 98 torpedoes for about Rs 2,012 crore. On 11$^{th}$ March 2013, the Defence Minister Mr A.K. Antony told the parliament, "Representations/references have been received from different quarters including from one competing vendor and Members of Parliament. Special Technical Oversight Committee (STOC) was constituted with approval of DAC (Defence Acquisition Council) to review the evaluation process and complaints received. The STOC has opined that the procurement has been progressed in accordance with the laid down procedures, in keeping with the provisions of the RFP (Request for Proposal) and DPP-06 (Defence procurement Policy) in transparent and fair manner. The DAC has considered the STOC Report and accepted the same in September 2012.

Government has not taken a final decision on the procurement." WASS is now banned from doing business with MoD. Atlas Elektronik SeaHake mod4 has been offered for the project.

The author attended the undocking of the first submarine at MDL yard no 11875 on 6$^{th}$ April 2015. The sub was loaded on a pontoon which was floating in a 10-meter deep area within the yard. The submarine's captain Cdr S.D. Mehendale was present at the undocking. The submarine will now undergo further outfitting in MDL's compound and finally floated in water in September 2015 during the launch. Post-launch, the sub will undergo further tests, including weapon release. Salient features of the undocking are:

- Weapon Launch Tubes, the core structure for the submarine's weapons arsenal (missiles & Torpedo's) installed and tested to withstand the pressure of 700-meter depth.
- The lifeline of the submarine "The High-Pressure Air System (250 Bar)" was installed 100%, and pressure testing in progress.
- The blood line of the submarine, "The Hydraulic system" installed 100% and one sub system out of 3, flushed with oil & pressure tested to 310 Bar.
- All propulsion machinery installed and "setting work" in progress.
- The propulsion shaft been installed.
- 9572 out of 10,000 meters of pipelines installed in the submarine and "setting work' is in advanced stage.
- 48,600 out of 50,000 meters of cabling installed

and "setting work" is in advanced stage.
- Main AC Switch Board & Secondary Switch Board (115V AC), supplying power to all weapon, sensors and control system, powering on complete.
- The nerve center of the submarine "Integrated Platform Management System (IPMS)" has been powered on. Setting work in progress.
- Connectors of all underwater pressure tight cables installed.
- All 165 Hull openings installed and pressure tested.
- Submarine vacuum test completed successfully ensuring water tightness of the submarine.
- All mast, attack periscope, search periscope, communication mast, radar mast, electronic support mast and snort mast installation completed.

The first submarine is to be named INS Kalvari post-commissioning. The rest of the five submarines are planned to be delivered every nine months after the September 2015 launch of Kalvari.

India is expected to exercise the four additional Scorpenes (P 75) option in Phase II of the 30-year submarine building plan after completing the hulls of the P - 75 (I) project. MDL's submarine hull making capacity is lying idle as the 6 P 75 hulls were completed a few years back.

# SUBMARINES AT WAR - 1971

*"The submarine will prevent any fleet remaining at sea continuously....it is astounding to me how the very best amongst us fail to recognise the vast impending revolution in naval warfare and naval strategy that the submarine will accomplish."*
**Admiral John Fisher**

The Indian Navy's fledgling submarine arm was faced with imminent war after the fourth Submarine INS Kursura reached the Indian shores. At the time, INS Kalvari was undergoing Medium Repairs at the Hindustan Shipyard Limited as she had nearly completed the first four years of her service and was long overdue for major refit and change in batteries.

The second submarine INS Khanderi operated as a training submarine with depth restrictions for a course under INS Virbahu. Like Kalvari, Khanderi had also nearly completed her first cycle of operational life and hence was not fully operational.

The third submarine INS Karanj had suffered an accident after surfacing under INS Ranjit and was undergoing repairs.

INS Kursura was the only fully operational Submarine under Captain A. Auditto. After being assigned to the West Coast, the submarine had already undergone a full work up with the Western fleet.

## 1971 War – West Coast

### INS Kursura

INS Kursura departed for operational patrols much before the war had begun. As per VAdm

Hiranandani's book 'Transition to Triumph', Kursura departed from Bombay on 13$^{th}$ November 1971 to reach her patrol location by 18$^{th}$ November. She remained there until 25$^{th}$ November, when she was shifted to a new patrol location and remained there until 30$^{th}$ November. On 30$^{th}$, she rendezvoused with INS Karanj at sea to transfer instructions and subsequently then left for Bombay and reached there by 4$^{th}$ December 1971. The mine laying operation by the submarine was cancelled.

RAdm A. Auditto (Retd), who was the submarine's captain then recalls in the 2010 edition of the naval magazine Periscope, "For Kursura a host of preparations were necessary at very short notice for proceeding on the War Patrol. This included embarking Torpedoes, Rations – deboned Mutton, and Chicken compressed into brick – shapes to be economically stored in the Deep Freeze compartment (it must be recollected that we had a large crew of 100 compared to about 45 in the HDWs!), specially preserved Bread etc. We had also arranged for loan of 4 nos. 16mm popular Hindi Films in reels with the projector which would occupy considerable space. Also suitable music, including march numbers by the Naval Band and patriotic songs were recorded on cassettes by my Electrical Officer. We had also two way communication codes to be used in case we had to break Radio silence for making Enemy Reports.

"We sailed from Bombay around midnight and were seen off by VAdm S.N. Kohli, FOC-in-C (W)- the first unit to proceed to War Station. We dived to periscope depth outside Bombay and headed for our patrol station. The next morning at 0800 we were surprised to receive a signal from FOC-in-C (W) calling for our PCS (a routine peacetime procedure ), we complied. At 2000 the same day we again received a PCS signal. Obviously the Indian naval communication centres (Comcen) had not shifted gear from 'Peacetime mode'. We replied-'PCS... do not intend breaking radio silence hereafter. The command remained worried as nothing was heard from us for the next 19 days till ordered to withdraw from our patrol station.

"Kursura proceeded to her patrol station without any untoward incident. We received regular bulletins about rumblings and political wrangling with our hostile neighbour. These news bulletins were received from Comcen and as per agreed procedure all signal messages for us were transmitted at high speed and repeated twice each day for two consecutive days. We could receive the message at periscope depth at the scheduled times depending on the tactical situation. No acknowledgement could be made as we were maintaining complete radio silence.

"While on patrol we had to remain at the best sonar listening depth in ultra-quiet state, except for a few hours at night to top up batteries. All except the duty watch had to rest in their bunks during the day. We had also to surface for a few minutes for astronomical fix at dawn and dusk if it was safe to do so.(no GPS in those early days !)

"All the routine activities were therefore concentrated during the hours of darkness, such as battery charging, ventilation, disposal of gash & sewage, cooking and partaking of meals.

"We had therefore staggered the Sub time by 12 hours so it would literally swap day and night.

This had to be done in stages over a period of

three days while transiting to the patrol area. As the crew would not see the light of day for the next two weeks we were on patrol, I thought that this change of time and routine would be easy.

"Each individual had to adjust the toilet timing according to his duty watch as the two toilets had to cater for 100. Water was rationed-half a bucket per head. The crew had to be kept engaged with quiz competitions, watching the four films over and over again, playing games like cards, ludo, carrom and of course listening to the taped music.

"Our orders were clear that in all cases we were to board and check the ship's papers for their identity and we were strictly prohibited from attacking any neutrals. This was an absurd situation which may have been prompted by the political leadership's fear of the reaction from neutrals and the inability of the navy to convince them that submarine ops demand bold offensive action. In any case the cause of an explosion in a tanker is impossible to identify if it has sunk.

"On the patrol we had two breakdowns firstly the Port Engine Exhaust Flap developed a leak and secondly the Hydraulic Hoist of the Radar Mast developed a defect. On each occasion we had to temporarily withdraw from our patrol station at night and proceed to the vicinity of the shipping lane, surface and send a team including the EO, the CHERA (Chief Engine Room Artificer) and casing hands to attend to these defects and return to the Patrol on rectification. On the 20$^{th}$ day of the Patrol we were ordered to withdraw from Patrol and hand over to Karanj. RV (rendezvous) was at 0800 . We approached the RV at periscope depth throwing off 10 degrees to Port to ensure that Karanj would be on our Stbd bow. At about 0730 the Sound Room reported an HE likely to be Karanj. Soon thereafter at 0805 we sighted Karanj on the surface. I presumed that she was unaware of our presence as she continued on her course neither did we get her radar on SHFDF. We proceeded towards her and when abreast of her, at half a cable, we surfaced. We exchanged Greetings and briefed the CO. Apparently their Cold Room compressor had packed up. We transferred ours by a jack stay. After that we wished them Good Luck and returned to Periscope depth for transit to Bombay."

### INS Karanj

INS Karanj commanded by Cdr V.S. Shekhawat (later Chief of Naval Staff) was deployed at Ormara, a port city in Makran Coast of restive Balochistan. Karanj's orders were similar to the ones given to Kursura.

The book 'No easy answers: the development of the navies of India, Pakistan, Bangladesh, and Sri Lanka, 1945-1996' by James Goldrick, states, "She made the rendezvous with Karanj on 2nd December to gather information on local conditions. Karanj sailed on 30th November as she was in her waiting station when war broke out. She closed into her patrol sector on 6th December and remained there until 14th December. Her presence, however, forced the Pakistanis to hug the coast inside the 15-fathom line and acted as a further restriction on the movements of the Pakistani surface fleet."

## 1971 War – East Coast

### INS Khanderi

On 28th November 1971, INS Khanderi sailed to the patrol area towards the south of the Eastern theatre of war. She was captained by Commander R.J. Milan and was under direct orders from C-in-C at Visakhapatnam. Her task was to patrol the area, which included the shipping route from Ceylon to Chittagong. She was tasked to sink Pakistani Naval and merchant ships and to collect information on Pakistani maritime forces. She came back to the harbour on 14th December 1971.

### INS Kalvari

As per the book 'No easy Answers', INS Kalvari was quickly reassembled and deployed to the base's northwest as a defensive measure in the absence of the Eastern Fleet's surface Forces.

Some interesting quotes related to the 1971 war from other books are mentioned below.

In the book `**No Way But Surrender - An Account of the Indo Pakistan War in the Bay of Bengal 1971**', VAdm N. Krishnan, then Flag Officer Commanding-in-Chief of the Eastern Naval Command, states, "One fleet submarine, KHANDERI was also to be mine. I felt that they were quite inadequate to fulfil the tasks ahead and also that we would be under-insuring the safety of the VIKRANT."

VAdm Hiranandani, in **Transition to Triumph,**

writes, "INS KHANDERI was sailed on 28 November 1971 to patrol an area across the shipping route from Ceylon to Chittagong. Her mission was:

(a) To destroy Pakistani naval ships.

(b) To destroy Pakistani merchant ships.

(c) To provide timely intelligence on Pakistani maritime forces.

Like her sister submarines off the West Coast of India, she was also tied down to the requirements of positive identification and informed that Pakistani merchantmen were masquerading as neutrals. Like the others, she also had an uneventful patrol and returned to harbour on 14th December 1971."

In '**We Dared: Maritime Operations in the 1971 Indo-Paк War**', Adm S.N. Kohli writes "The Western Fleet was given a broad directive to seek and destroy enemy warships, protect our merchant shipping, deny sealanes to enemy shipping and render ineffective the maritime line of communication between West Pakistan and East Pakistan to prevent any reinforcements from reaching the beleaguered Pakistani forces at that end.

"A submarine patrol was to be instituted off Karachi to sink their warships and merchant ships proceeding to Karachi."

## *SUBMARINE OPERATIONS*

Western Naval Command was allocated two submarines KURSURA and KARANJ, operating directly under FOCINCWEST. Since the approaches to Karachi and the Makran Coast were going to be transited by the Western Fleet and by the submarines, waiting stations and submarine havens were established. To exclude any possibility of mistaken identity, two precautions were taken:

(a) Corridors were demarcated which were not to be crossed.

(b) Submarines were required to positively identify a target before attack."

Page 82 - KURSURA's Patrol

"KURSURA was deployed on patrol during the precautionary stage, before the outbreak of hostilities. The aims of the patrol were:

(a) To attack and sink all Pakistani warships.

(b) To sink all merchant shipping sighted/detected when specifically ordered.

(c) Patrol and surveillance.

"A waiting station and two patrol areas were established. The submarine was to proceed to her waiting station prior to the commencement of hostilities and move into her patrol area only after receiving a signal `Commence hostilities with Pakistan'. She sailed from base port on 13$^{th}$ November 1971 and arrived in her waiting station in the forenoon of 18 November. She stayed on patrol in her waiting station till 25$^{th}$ November. Thereafter, she was shifted to another area where she remained till 30$^{th}$ November. On 30$^{th}$ November, she was ordered to R/V KARANJ at sea to pass necessary information and instructions which she did and thereafter she entered Bombay on 4$^{th}$ December.

"She encountered a number of tankers in her waiting station, and two or three commercial aircraft daily on international routes. She had fair weather throughout."

*KARANJ's Patrol*
""KARANJ, with orders similar to KURSURA, sailed on 30$^{th}$ November 1971 for her patrol. She effected R/V with KURSURA at sea on 2$^{nd}$ December 1971 and thereafter proceeded to her waiting station which she entered at 1600 hrs on 3$^{rd}$ December. The same night, she received information that hostilities with Pakistan had broken out. She was, however, ordered to remain in her waiting station. On 5$^{th}$ December at 0145 hrs she received orders to move to her patrol area which she entered on the morning of 6$^{th}$ December. On transit she received news of the Fleet's bombardment of Karachi and the sinking of two PN warships. Morale on board was high.

"The Commanding Officer, traversed the entire patrol area assigned to the submarine. His deductions at the end of it were:

(a) Upto 8$^{th}$ December. Ships were using the normal shipping route traversing the route east of Ormara by night. Air recce was `moderate' east of Ormara and `slight' west of it. Warship activity was `slight'.

(b) On the night of 8/9 December. Hectic aerial recce and warship activity to the west, north-west and south-west of Cape Monze. Radio Pakistan announced a hunt for an Indian submarine off their coast.

(c) 9/10 December and thereafter. All shipping traffic moved inside the 10 to 15 fathom line along the Makran coast. Warship activity frequent in Sonmiani Bay and off Ormara but close to the coast. Intense aerial recce east and south of Ormara from Monze and following the same route while approaching from the south.

(d) 11 to 14 December. No shipping activity west of Ormara. Intense aerial activity east of Ormara and moderate to the west. Some warship activity possible near Ormara.

"On the evening of 14$^{th}$ December, the submarine was directed to withdraw from her patrol and she returned to base port on 20$^{th}$ December 1971.

"KARANJ thus became the longest deployed naval unit during the 1971 Indo-Pak conflict. She had been out from 30$^{th}$ November to 20$^{th}$ December 1971. On four different occasions during this patrol, the submarine almost released her weapons on merchantmen. The requirement to positively identify these precluded any firings."

**Lack of Kills**

The 1971 hostiles saw unparalleled naval warfare like the missile boat attack on Karachi, devastation caused by the aircraft carrier on the eastern front and others. However, the Indian submarines could not find an opportunity to score a kill resulting in a debate over the employment of submarines in future. Naval leadership assigns the pre-condition for positive identification as the main reason for the lack of kills.

To set the record straight, both the political and naval leadership are to be equally held responsible for the pre-condition. The political leadership was apprehensive of dragging the neutral countries into the war and hence asked for positive identification of the targets before sinking them. The naval leadership was to blame itself for instituting the concept of positive identification.

Cmde R.S. Vasan (Retd) writes in the 2013 edition of Quarter Deck, "The concept of submarine operations and the challenges of operating in patrol areas close to the enemy shores was brought out by Cmde Subra-Manian. It was also brought out that the rules of engagement that were in force did not allow any attacks until a positive identification was established of own submarine was under attack. With limitations of the Foxtrot class, this was indeed a tall order, particularly when someone has to be positively identified. Cmde Subra-Manian also brought out the lessons for the navy of future in terms of conducting such operation." It is important to mention that Cmde Subra-Manian served submarines for only 5-6 years.

Some naval analysts speak about the lack of training and inferiority of Foxtrots vis-vis the Pakistani Agosta submarines during the war. It is agreed that the submarine arm was new and was primarily used for surveillance and Anti-Submarine Warfare (ASW) training. But since the submarines were deployed primarily for anti-shipping roles and not hunter-killer missions against enemy submarines, lack of training and inferior submarines is irrelevant.

"Submarine operations involve a complex array of specific skills such as Sonar Analysis, tactical appreciation, building combat proficiency, handling submarine weapons, Submarine platform management etc. These groups, once proficient in their domains, need to seamlessly integrate as an efficient combat team. Submarining Ethos is developing and sustaining these proficiencies. Experience gained, lessons learnt are translated to Standard Operating Procedures and the constant honing of skills learning the value of SOPs and then pushing the operating, safety, and tactical envelopes is what makes efficient submarine operations. This takes time. Peace time exercises inspections workups are all designed to provide training and opportunity to develop submarining skills," explains VAdm K.N. Sushil (Retd).

The submarines were not mere onlookers during the war. They performed the role of sea denial during the war and managed to bottle up the Pakistani naval fleet in the harbor.

# SUBMARINE ACCIDENTS

*" Submarines are safe till you forget that they can be dangerous "*

**Opening sentence of Submarine Standing Orders**

Like any other mode of transport, the submarines can meet with accidents, but they normally capture worldwide attention. The U.S. Navy, which operates a fleet of 71 submarines, reports approximately 60 - 150 accidents per year. Russian Navy Kursk and Indian Navy INS Sindhurakshak are the most fatal submarine accidents of recent years. Serving the submarines is a risky profession, and hence it is a volunteer arm of the Indian Navy.

Indian submarines often collide with ships while surfacing or at periscope depth. A layman wonders why the submarines do not collide in the depths but collide while surfacing. The submarines do not collide in the depths because they are constantly listening on passive sonar. Since there is no vertical sonar for surfacing, the subs transmit on active sonar located in the head sector to detect a surface contact. However, on occasions, a contact may not get picked up, and if then, while breaking to periscope depth, something happens to be on top, a collision could occur. Sometimes the surface ships are unaware of the submarine's presence at periscope level and damage the periscope while moving over it.

Below is a list of known accidents involving Indian navy submarines.

### *INS Karanj – INS Ranvir*

In 1970, INS Karanj, whilst dived at Periscope depth,

suffered a collision with the 1700 ton destroyer INS Ranjit, off Cochin. Ranjit had to be towed back to the harbour and, Karanj returned back under her own power. After the repairs, the reconstructed bridge of Karanj was not exactly aligned fore and aft, writes VAdm A.K. Singh, who served as the submarines' navigator and XO, in the naval magazine Periscope.

### *INS Vela – INS Rana*

INS Vela had dived after its fin hit INS Rana in December 1989. INS Rana (D115) was a Rajput Class destroyer was acquired in 1949 from the Royal Navy. INS Vela made it back to port under own power.

### *INS Sindhughosh - Merchant Ship*

On 10$^{th}$ January 2008, Frontier India had reported the collision of INS Sindhughosh with a merchant ship. Soon, the experts began blaming the Indian sonar USHUS for the accident. The report stated, "INS Sindhughosh is reported to collided with a merchant ship damaging some part of the conning tower. INS Sindhughosh was taking part in Fleet Level war games and was at periscope level."

Sindhughosh sailed back to sea after three months of the accident, and it was revealed that the merchant ship hit the Submarine and not vice versa.

### INS Sindhuratna and INS Sindhukesri

INS Sindhuratna and INS Sindhukesri collided on 3$^{rd}$ July 2010, when they were alongside each other while entering the narrow gateway to the naval dockyard. Both vessels were lucky to survive the hit as the pressurised double-hull could absorb most of the impact, but the rudder of one of the submarines was damaged. At the time, one submarine was docked while the other was being towed alongside it. The damage was minimal because of the low speed. The Kilo-class attack submarines were returning to the harbour after a reconnaissance and patrol mission off the city harbour when the incident occurred.

### *INS Sindhurakshak Battery Explosion*

In February 2010, INS Sindhurakshak had suffered a fire due to a battery explosion resulting in 1 causality. She was berthed in Visakhapatnam at the time of the accident.

Sindhurakshak has just returned from Russia after a major refit at Russia's Zvezdochka shipyard.

### *INS Sindhurakshak Explosion and sinking*

On 14th August 2013, the Indian Navy Kilo-class Submarine INS Sindhurakshak (S63) suffered an explosion that caused a major fire on board. The submarine had submerged with a small portion visible above the surface. The submarine was in its berth, and about 18 persons were onboard the submarine at the time of the accident.

A navy release said the incident occurred shortly after midnight on the 14th. Naval and Mumbai Fire brigade fire tenders had reached the scene, and the fire has been brought under control.

Due to proximity, INS Sindhugosh too suffered damages due to the explosion. Usually, submarines are berthed in pairs at Naval Dockyard.

In June 2014, Sindhurakshak was recovered on even-keel (right side up) with the help of the Dutch marine salvage company Smit International. The innards were found melted or burned. The probable cause of the explosion is said to be the torpedo.

The submarine has been decommissioned, and the navy is yet to take a call on its future disposal.

### *INS Sindhuratna – Smoke onboard*

On 26th February 2014, smoke was detected in INS Sindhuratna, leading to the evacuation of 5 personnel while two others were missing. Sindhuratna was at sea off Mumbai for routine training and workup (inspection). While at sea in the early hours, smoke was reported in the sailors' accommodation in compartment number three. Smoke was brought under control by the submarine crew, and in the process, seven crew members had inhaled smoke and felt uneasy. The submarine was not carrying any weapons onboard.

The Headquarters, Western Naval Command (HQ WNC), rushed a Seaking Helicopter with a medical team to evacuate the seven crew members who were then transferred to Naval Hospital INHS Asvini. Naval ships were also dispatched to provide assistance to the submarine.

On 27th, Sindhuratna docked in the Mumbai Naval dockyard. A high-level inquiry, headed by an officer of Rear Admiral rank, was constituted to ventilate the submarine, establish the cause of the incident, and recommend steps for continuing safe operations of submarines.

The two missing officers Lt Commander Kapish Muwal and Lt Manoranjan Kumar, were confirmed dead as they were trapped in the submarine battery compartment, which is the third compartment. The compartment had sealed automatically after the smoke was detected. The compartment doors were not opened manually as it would have affected the rest of the 90 odd crew in the submarine. Navy Chief Admiral D.K. Joshi resigned after the accident.

### INS Sindhughosh - Fishing Boat

On the night of 21$^{st}$ February 2015, a fishing boat hit the periscope of INS Sindhughosh while it was at manoeuvres during naval exercise Tropex (Theatre Readiness Operational Level Exercise) in the Arabian Sea.

Times of India quoted an official who explained the reason for the accident. "The submarine was practising 'special boat section' operation during which divers swim out of its torpedo tubes with a Gemini boat to carry out a covert land operation on land. It was pitch-dark when the operation was being carried out close to the coastline, south of Mumbai," said an official.

"The fishing boat hit the submarine's periscope without any warning. The submarine surfaced and then made its way to the naval dockyard at Mumbai, where its damaged periscope will be repaired. It's an occupational hazard, but such exercises have to be carried out," he added.

### When does a submarine sink?

A submarine can sink only if it suffers a loss of buoyancy due to physical damage either due to collision or flooding in the pressure hull. As long as this does not happen touching bottom etc. are incident occurrences that are not counted as accidents. In fact, most conventional submarines are designed to sit at the bottom to conserve power. In the operational cycle, each sub is tasked to carry out a bottoming exercise.

The Russian submarines are far more insured against sinkability compared to the western designs. This is because, traditionally, they are double-hulled. The pressure hull is saddled with the outer hull, and in between are the ballast tanks. The total volume of the ballast tanks is called the reserve buoyancy, which in the case of Russian submarines is about 25-30 %, whereas, in the case of western designs, it is only 10%.

Usually, the unsinkability of a Russian boat is that even if one compartment with the ballast tanks saddling it is damaged, the boat can still surface. She would not dive thereafter till the damage is repaired. When we say 10 or 30 % or the proportion of the water tight volume, which is the volume of the pressure hull in most cases, but in Kilo's, the volume of the sonar capsule is also included being water tight.

In western designs, the ballast tanks are not saddled but buttoned onto the forward and aft ends. It is for this reason that a Russian boat is also safer in respect of a torpedo hit. It may damage the outer hull and the ballast tanks only.

**Submarine safety**

In view of the recent incident with submarines, the navy instituted safety stand-downs and extensive checks for weapon-related safety systems and audit of Standard Operating Procedures. Navy's regulations prescribe any incident is thoroughly investigated to identify any errors and, more importantly, to address critical areas on material and training related aspects to prevent recurrence of incidents. The outcome of the analysis was promulgated to the submarine training establishments and operational authorities for corrective measures.

In addition, the NHQ directed the conduct of safety 'stand-down' and one-time safety audits prior to the operational deployment of any ship or submarine. The procedures involve 'Safety Audits' of all operational units by nominated teams at the command and operational levels. Safety templates to undertake these audits were promulgated. A feedback procedure has also been institutionalised and is being monitored at Naval Headquarters.

The Kilo-class and the Shishumar class lack fixed on-board health monitoring systems that can alert technicians ashore to sub-par performance of equipment and systems, signalling potential breakdown. Periodic checks are carried out using a portable monitoring system comprising a network of sensors, but are only possible when the submarine is at the harbour. There is a laid down inspection schedule. As per the norms, the pumps and motors are to be health-checked every six months, while propulsion systems need a thorough inspection every quarter.

In view of the above, the DRDO has announced the development of a system to conduct a structured health monitoring of the under-development nuclear submarines and future conventional submarines of the navy. The system works on the philosophy of predictive (prognosis-driven) maintenance and has been installed on the first indigenous nuclear submarine INS Arihant.

# MIDGETS AND CHARIOTS

Pakistan had acquired midgets and Chariots by 1967 for its special operation forces. During the 1971 war, the Indian Navy had anticipated attacks by the midgets, but the fear was unfounded as the Pakistanis could not field the midgets and Chariots due to shortage of spares and unsuitability of the midgets to fire torpedoes.

> Military submarines weighing less than 150 tonnes are called midgets. The civilian version and non-combat versions are generally referred to as submersibles. Working with mother ships or submarines, the midgets are capable of carrying up to 8 personnel and can be configured to fire weapons, deliver personnel covertly or gather intelligence. A 'Chariot' is an underwater two-man swimmer delivery vehicle of Italian make. The Chariots are reported to have the ability to carry a mine with 230 kilograms of explosives and two divers up to 50 nautical miles.

In the 1970s, the navy began creating Deep Diving specialisation within the Diving Cadre. Two officers, Lt Vimal Kumar (later Cmde) and Lt H.S. Dhingra, later (LCdr), were deputed to the Soviet Union for the Deep Diving course. The submarine rescue vessel INS Nistar acted as a mother ship for the divers. During the 1971 war, the diver shortage was felt, and after the war, the navy began expanding the force.

In September 1972, a naval delegation went to Italy to acquire midget submarines and Chariots from the same Italian firm which had previously supplied the equipment to the Pakistani Navy in 1967. They found the midget unsuitable for long-range operations in tropical waters, difficult to man, and uncertain maintainability. However, the delegation found the Chariots useful, and six were ordered. The acceptance trials were conducted in 1974, and the six units reached Bombay in 1975.

The first replacement crew for the Chariots were trained by 1976. On 01$^{st}$ May 1980, a newly built chariot complex was commissioned as INS Abhimanyu. The Chariots were used to asses defensive measures for offshore oil-producing rigs at Bombay High against attack by Pakistani Navy midgets and exercise ships in harbour in Operation AWKWARD (defence against underwater divers) procedures. The chariots could also be operationally deployed when required. Since the submarine tender INS Amba was rebased to Bombay to support the Vela class submarines, the navy decided to use it for the deployment of the Chariots too.

One Chariot was displayed on IMS Vikrant (former Aircraft carrier, then museum ship, now scrapped) in 2011. As per the authors' interaction with naval personnel deputed on the museum ship, the navy had procured CE2F/X100 version from Cos.Mos. Spa, Italy. X100 refers to operations up to 100 meters underwater. The marine commandos are trained on chariots, and there are approximately five units existing. The Chariots are not considered outdated by the users.

It is possible that the navy may acquire Chariot sized vessels 'commando containers.' In 2014, Larsen & Toubro had displayed a two man container in-house design similar to the Chariots.

# Foxtrot to Arihant

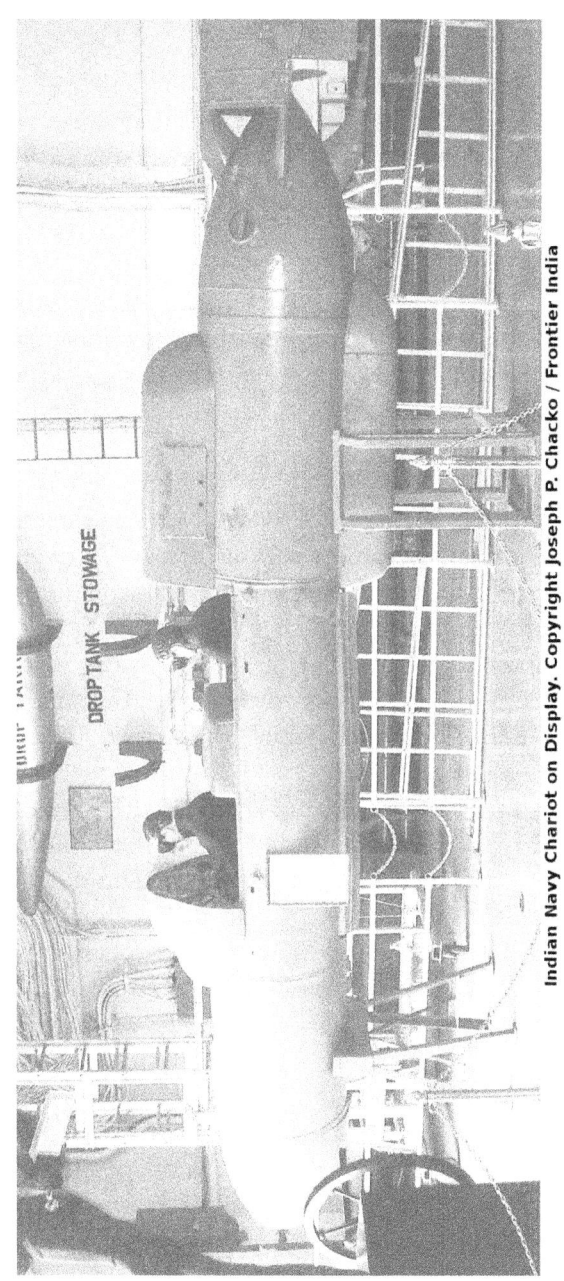

Indian Navy Chariot on Display. Copyright Joseph P. Chacko / Frontier India

## Midgets

The Indian Navy is of the view that improvised mini-submarines may emerge as the primary threat for Indian maritime security. The threat could range from manned or unmanned military midgets or the ones employed for recreational scuba diving. These submersibles are capable of attacking Indian warships, important port infrastructure, lay mines and deliver special operation forces. Their detection is difficult due to the complex and cluttered sonar picture in shallow tropical waters.

The 26/11 terror strikes in Mumbai led to the dusting of the nearly 45-year-old project of inducting the midgets and became a part of the navy's efforts to strengthen its underwater operational capabilities.

On 01$^{st}$ November 2009, PTI reported on the navy's plans to acquire five midgets to strengthen the underwater capabilities of the Marine Commandos (MARCOS). Quoting defence ministry sources, the report said that the process of acquiring the vessels had begun with Requests for Proposals (RFP) issued to Indian shipyards, including Hindustan Shipyards Limited, ABG and Pipavav shipyards. The navy was planning to procure five midgets and double the number if required later. The midget is designed to carry four to six personnel on board, with a diving depth of around 400m. The midgets will have the capability of carrying out both manned and unmanned operations and will be equipped with a host of weapons including torpedoes. They would also be capable of being launched independently or being attached with larger mother submarines.

On 16$^{th}$ November 2012, a tender was floated by

the government for the supply of swimmer delivery vehicles (SDV) and commando containers. The Defence Acquisition Council gave the clearance to acquire two mini submersibles - special operations boats/swimmer delivery vehicle (SOB/SDV) on 25$^{th}$ October 2014. The specifications stated were different compared to the PTI report above. The Tribune reported that the midgets will be 16-20m long and carry 10-12 armed troops.

The construction of the midgets were subsequently awarded to the Indian Defence Public Sector unit Hindustan Shipyard Ltd (HSL ) at a cost of approximately Rs.3,000 crore. "We are expecting to ground work on the project by completing all the procedures by the year-end and deliver it in three years," HSL Chairman and Managing Director RAdm N.K. Mishra (Retd) told The Hindu on 09$^{th}$ February 2015. The SDV can accommodate eight personnel, including two pilot crews, reports the paper.

Joseph P. Chacko

# NUCLEAR SUBMARINES FOR INDIA – HISTORICAL PERSPECTIVE

> Although VAdm Hiranandani traces India's earliest nuclear propulsion ambitions to the 1960s, there is evidence that the naval planners have had thoughts of acquiring SSN's in the 1950s. This is discussed in the chapter on indigenous SSGN's.

In his book ' Transition to Triumph, nuclear propulsion has been considered for the ships as early as 1964 by Dr. Homi Bhabha and pursued by his successors, writes VAdm Hiranandani. The intention of the navy to create nuclear-propelled submarines goes back to 1967. The first feasibility studies were initiated in 1968-69 at the Bhabha Atomic Research Centre (BARC), writes Anil Anand, who headed the team building the nuclear reactor for the Indian nuclear submarine, in his book 'The Second Strike'. Two engineers from the navy, Gurmeet Singh and V.K. Chadha, joined the BARC training school in 1968. There were others from the Navy who followed later. After the initial training, they were sent back to the naval service.

In 1976 the Committee of Secretaries approved a project codenamed the 'Plutonium Recycling Plant' (Plutonium Recycling Project - Land-based prototype propulsion plant) to be set up by the navy in association with the BARC.

After the approval, the navy began sending its teams to the BARC for the reactor design. "The naval teams began arriving at the BARC in 1976," writes

Cmde Ranjit B. Rai (Retd) in the magazine 'India Strategic'. "Dr. Homi Sethna, as the Chairman of the Atomic Energy Commission (AEC), opened the secret portals of India's nuclear establishment at BARC to a team of four naval officers led by then Captains P.N. Agarwala and Bharat Bhusan, both very bright engineer officers trained at the Royal Naval Engineering College at Manadon Plymouth. The two others were Commander Gurmit Singh and Commander B.K. Subbarao, and in the later years' Commander Subbarao also prepared a design for a submarine nuclear power plant" adds Cmde Rai. Anil Anand confirms it in his book, "in 1976, a team from the navy under Captain P.N. Agrawal and later Captain B. Bhushan was posted in BARC under the overall guidance of Dr. Pranab Rebatiranjan Dastidar, Director of the Reactor group, to be trained and study various design options with the help of BARC".

B.P. Rastogi, S.K. Mehta, L.G.K. Murthy, B.F. Chamany, S. Seshadri and P.R. Roy were among the scientists and engineers from the BARC who participated in evaluating various options and changing parameters based on the input for future users.

India also approached the Soviet Union for suggestions on acquiring nuclear submarines. Speaking at the India International Trade center in 2005, Former Prime Minister Mr. I.K. Gujral shared an anecdote relevant to the Indian Navy's plans and ambitions to possess nuclear submarines with underwater launched long-range missiles. Mr. Gujral revealed how in 1979 when he was Ambassador in Russia and Mr. C. Subramaniam and Mr. K. Subrahmanyam were the Defence Minister and

Defence Secretary (Production) respectively in MOD, he was tasked to meet Admiral of the Fleet of the Soviet Union Sergey Georgiyevich Gorshkov and seek help and guidance on India's quest for nuclear submarines. The duo, in turn, was prompted by the Indian Navy and supported by Dr. Raja Ramanna. Admiral Gorshkov, known to be a supporter of the Indian Navy and officially acknowledged as the 'Benefactor of the modern Indian Navy', was one of the finest naval minds of the last century. When Mr. Gujral met him, Admiral Gorshkov made him look at the chart/map of the Indian Ocean and went on to explain how India was hemmed in by the Straits on both sides and said China has nuclear submarines, and so India must also have atomic submarines. That was the time when relations between Russia and China had soured. (Source: 12 March 2005, indiadefence.com).

Former Defence Minister Mr. George Fernandes mentions another instance of Soviet opinion over the subject during Mr. Gujral's tenure in Moscow. "Former Soviet head, Nikita Khruschev had told Gujral in Moscow that China had nuclear submarines, and he was sure they were not planning to attack Australia….In 1979, the Chinese had 20 nuclear submarines." (Source: May 1998, Rediff).

The Soviet Union offered to lease a nuclear submarine to India in 1981. Marshal Nikolai Ogarkov made the offer during his visit to India in April 1981 writes the former President, Mr. R. Venkataraman, in his book 'My Presidential Years'. The Soviets offered to arrange a two-year training programme for Indian naval personnel, lease one nuclear submarine for 5 years for practical training, and render technical assistance for creating maintenance facilities in India for nuclear-powered submarines. He added that the sale as also assistance for designing and constructing nuclear-powered submarines could be taken up later.

VAdm M. K. Roy, in his book 'War in the Indian Ocean', describes an interesting set of events on the Indian side following the offer. Mrs. Indira Gandhi, the defence minister, conveyed the proposal to the Chief of Naval Staff, Adm R. L. Pereira, who rejected it on two grounds. Adm Pereira believed that it was a ploy to scuttle the HDW deal, which was near finalization, and India could not afford nuclear submarines. He felt that it would neither strengthen the navy's submarine arm nor add muscle to India's maritime forces. But Mrs. Gandhi had already approved the order to buy two HDW-1500 submarines and construct two more at MDL. She consulted Dr. Raja Ramanna, the distinguished nuclear scientist, the Scientific Advisor to the Defence Minister, Director General of DRDO and Secretary to Government for Defence Research. Dr. Ramanna, in turn, contacted his old friend VAdm Mihir Roy in Eastern Naval Command.

VAdm Roy further writes that on one occasion in 1974, when he was a Captain and commanded the aircraft carrier INS Vikrant, spoke on the need to go nuclear, and Dr. Ramanna had remained unusually quiet. VAdm Mihir Roy was now the C-in-C of Eastern Naval Command and hence the Submarine-Operating Authority, and his opinion was vital.

The issue came up for discussion during the Commanders Conference at Visakhapatnam, which began shortly after. The proceedings began with the agenda that "the Indian Navy should not support the proposal for nuclear submarine acquisition as it was not necessary and the navy lacked the resources and manpower for the same". Adm Pereira said the government had nominated Dr. Raja Ramanna led delegation to Moscow to discuss the Soviet offer, and VAdm Roy was included in the delegation. Expressing his view, VAdm Roy said that the navy should analyse the pros and cons before arriving at a decision. Fleet Commander RAdm Kewal Krishan Nayyar too supported VAdm Roy's argument.

The Soviet Defence Minister Marshal Ustinov reiterated the offer to lease a nuclear submarine in March 1982. Venkataraman met up with Marshal Ustinov, who was in Delhi, and during the meeting, the Marshal expressed all support for inducting nuclear-powered submarines with conventional weapons into the Indian Navy.

On the indigenous reactor front, VAdm Roy writes in Naval Quarterdeck that the BARC and Navy team submitted a detailed report in 1980 with uranium as the fuel (instead of plutonium). Anil Anand states that the final report was submitted in 1983, which led to a final decision to proceed with the project. The naval team soon left the BARC as their job was complete. One of the decision outcomes was the establishment of an organization called Advanced Technology Vessel (ATV).

## The case of Dr B.K. Subbarao

The story of an Indian nuclear submarine reactor is incomplete without mentioning Dr. Buddhi Kota Subbarao, a naval scientist who was allegedly framed, imprisoned for 20 months, dragged in a five-year case and finally acquitted.

The BARC created the first nuclear submarine propulsion plant design, which had to be dropped in 1976 after Commander B. K. Subbarao gave a report on his technical findings. The second design also had to be dropped in January 1978 as Cdr Subbarao proved that it was unsuitable for naval application. Upset BARC designers bypassed the naval team and submitted the third design directly to Prime Minister Indira Gandhi in mid-1980. The budget for building a prototype was estimated at approximately Rs. 150 Crore. Mrs. Gandhi sought Cdr Subbarao's technical opinion via the defence minister R. Venkatraman. Cdr Subbarao pointed out to the lack of basic standards like safety standards followed by such designs in other nuclear navies. Mrs. Gandhi returned the BARC proposal but with a clause for reconsideration if the BARC team can refute Cdr Subbarao's claim. As BARC worked on a fourth design, the navy asked Cdr Subbarao to work on a design that was submitted to PM's office towards the end of 1982. Cdr Subbarao was recalled to active naval service after BARC allegedly pressured the navy to withdraw him from the PRP.

The matter did not end there. In 1985, Cdr Subbarao acquired a PhD from the Indian Institute of Technology, Bombay, based on his thesis "Nuclear Power Plant Modelling and Design Multivariable Control Approach". Subsequently, he took voluntary retirement from the navy in October 1987. As per open sources, Gopi Krishna Arora, the Secretary of Information and Broadcasting, relayed to Dr. Subbarao an offer by the then Prime Minister Rajiv Gandhi, to be the Technical Head of the nuclear submarine project. Dr. Subbarao was unsatisfied as he was appointed by an executive order, rather than a Selection Committee, which could also scrutinise other scientists. The idea allegedly alarmed the BARC team working on the project and conspired against him. He was charged and arrested for smuggling of secret documents out of the country under the Official Secrets Act and the Atomic Energy Act, as he reached the Sahar Airport to visit USA to make a presentation for a joint venture between CEAT (INDIA) and AT&T (USA).

India Testfires K/15/ BO-5 Missile from underwater pantoon

# LEASED NUCLEAR SUBS - INS CHAKRA

## Charlie-I Class

Soon after Marshal Ogarkov's offer, Dr. Ramanna, VAdm Roy and RAdm Biloo Choudhry (Director of Marine Engineering) visited the Soviet Union twice to discuss the possibility of lease of a nuclear submarine.

During the first visit in July 1981, the Indian team was given a walk around an old Victor class attack submarine in the port city of Murmansk, in northwest Russia. Dr. Pranab Rebatiranjan Dastidar, the electronics expert at the BARC, was also present during the event. After coming back to Moscow, the Indian team expressed the need for a less noisy submarine due to the presence of more sophisticated NATO Submarines in the Indian Ocean Region.

The initial talks were concretised on 14th April 1982 as an 'Inter-Governmental Agreement of consent in principle' embodying the initial offer for training, leasing and assistance in constructing the base and operational facilities for a nuclear submarine in India was signed by Dr. Ramanna and Admiral Gorshkov. Admiral Gorshkov stated that the sub would not come under International Atomic Energy Association (IAEA) safeguards as it was not a weapon but only a propulsion system.

Meanwhile, Mr. Venkataraman became the defence minister, and Dr. V.S Arunachalam replaced Dr. Ramanna. VAdm Roy was shifted to the MOD in the capacity of Secretary to Government to negotiate multiple agreements and finalize the costs for training and the lease terms for the nuclear submarine. VAdm

Roy visited the Soviet Union numerous times along with delegations to complete and sign the working protocols for the induction of a nuclear submarine into the Indian Navy.

In May 1982, the assembling and screening of the naval personnel who would operate the nuclear submarine began at INS Hamla the Logistics Training Establishment of the navy located in the city of Bombay. Two and a half crews were carefully selected after the necessary psychological aptitude tests.

Following a Russian language course in Bombay, two weeks' escape course was conducted for the naval crew at submarine training establishment INS Satavahana in February 1983.

The officers were originally scheduled to depart for the erstwhile Soviet Union by the end of March 1983, but there was some delay in receiving the movement orders. The wait was due to the uncertainty of whether the families would be allowed to accompany them. This caused anxiety among the crew members as some of them had sold their house and belongings and were waiting for their orders. The officers and families finally left on 28th September by a chartered plane for Vladivostok, the largest Russian port on the Pacific Ocean, via Tashkent.

There were eight bachelors among the team of 60 officers who reached Vladivostok on 30th September under the command of Cmde Sam Daniel, who was to be the Officer in charge of the detachment for the next 30 Months. The bachelors were put up in a hostel close to the training centre and families in a 12 storey building in the Sovetskie region in the greater municipal limits of Vladivostok close to 'Vtoraya Rechka' or the Second river. The officers were given

3-bedroom, 2-bedroom, and studio flats, which were allotted based on seniority and family size. The apartments were furnished. The first, sixth and twelfth floors were allocated to the Russian staff attached with the Indian crew.

The officers arrived at the Training Centre at Vladivostok on 1$^{st}$ October for a 30-month course. The training Centre was located 20 km from their Kirova Street residential quarters on the territory of the local Submarine base at Bay 'Malie Uliss' or small Uliss in the region Churkin.

The Indian Navy officers travelled to the base daily at 0745 to reach the Centre by 0830. Thereafter they would draw their books from the secret library for the classes, which started at 0900. The session went on till 1400 when they had a break for lunch. At 1530, the officers began their self-study period till 1800. On returning the books to the library, the return road journey would start and reach by 1915. This routine was followed during the entire theoretical training of 18 months. The language course was for four months, and officers were divided into six groups based on rank and specialisation.

In December 1983, a team led by the Soviet Minister of Ship-Building and specialists arrived in India to assess the Indian industrial expertise and competence to handle a nuclear submarine.

The remaining crew arrived from India on 28$^{th}$ January 1984. They were put up in a hostel along with the bachelor officers close to the Training Centre. This hostel building, called the ZBK, had two wings. One a five-storey one where the sailors were billeted and on the ground floor was the dining hall for meals and a two-storey one where the bachelor officers were billeted and also housed the administrative offices of the detachment.

The 12-month technical course for officers started in February 1984. Sailors' language course started at the same time followed by technical course for eight months. In March 1985, an escape course was conducted for the entire crew.

An agreement was finalised for the transfer of a nuclear submarine to India during the visit of then Indian Prime Minister Rajiv Gandhi to Moscow in May 1985 (South Asia's Nuclear Security Dilemma: India, Pakistan, and China, Lowell Dittmer). By 1985, when Mr. P. V. Narasimha Rao (who was the Minister of Defence - 31$^{st}$ December 1984 to 25$^{th}$ September 1985) visited the Soviet Union, rumours were thick about the probable Soviet offer of a nuclear-powered submarine to India to counter Pakistan's Agosta class submarine.

The crew had further practical training on board a Submarine for another 12 months. The Soviets had used a Charlie-l Class nuclear submarine at Uliss Bay as part of the Sea training programme. At first, the Indian crew would embark on watches, and the Russian Crew would be fully in charge. Progressively Indian crew numbers increased, and the Russian crew reduced till they were embarked in watches and a complete Indian crew was onboard.

During the training, the crew fired 42 practice torpedoes and three 'Amethist' missiles with a range of 70 km. Amethist was an intelligent missile specially designed against a U.S. Carrier Battle Group and had a logic to hit the centre of the formation for bearing as well as range.

The Indian ambassador Professor Nurul Hasan

visited the Indian crew in July 1985. The graduation ceremony was conducted in April 1986, and the crews were sent back to India.

The Soviet Union faced worldwide opposition against the intended nuclear submarine transfer. Within the Soviet Union, some officials were worried over the new arms race in the Indian Ocean, violation of the Nuclear proliferation Treaty (NPT), falling of the Soviet reactor technology into American hands and the possibility that the Americans might make a similar transfer to the Pakistanis as a retaliation.

In October 1986, the Soviet Politburo reiterated their earlier decision to transfer a Charlie-I class submarine to India for three years for training purposes. The Soviets also took measures to develop safeguards to minimise possible compromise of Soviet propulsion technology.

For secrecy, the submarine was code-named 877S. Since India was already on the verge of purchasing the EKM 877 Kilo submarines from the Soviets, the designation 877 would not raise suspicion. The designation S was for special project.

Captain R. N. Ganesh who was among the first batch of trainees for the nuclear submarine, Commanders R. K. Shanna (executive officer), B.R. Raju (nuclear engineering), P. K. Sharma (electrical engineering) and Arun Kumar (First lieutenant and Operations Officer), along with one complete Indian crew were back to Uliss Bay on 8$^{th}$ August 1987.

A refurbished SSGN Charlie-I was transferred to the Indian Navy on 05$^{th}$ January 1988. The commissioning was to take place in November 1987. The boat was to reach Visakhapatnam by 20th November, before Admiral R.H. Tahiliani handed over the reins of the navy to Admiral J.G. Nadkarni. However, the commissioning was postponed due to the Intermediate-Range Nuclear Forces Treaty (INF) talks scheduled between the U.S and Soviet Union in November 1987. Ultimately, it took place on 5$^{th}$ January 1988.

The refresher course for the Indian crew was conducted for 30 days, followed by ten days for storing and five days for acceptance trials. The submarine was armed with Eight P-70 Ametist Cruise missiles (NATO reporting name SS-N-7 Starbright, GRAU designation 4K66) with 70 km range. After the submarine's commissioning in Vladivostok, the command and control were vested in the Indian Navy.

INS Chakra - Charlie 1

With the commissioning of INS Chakra (S71), India entered the elite club of six countries operating nuclear-powered submarines. In the history of international cooperation, the act of leasing out a nuclear submarine was unprecedented. It was the first time a nuclear submarine was ever transferred to any other country.

The run-up to clinching the deal in the Cold War era was no less than a diplomatic feat and spoke volumes about the strong strategic ties between India and the Soviet Union. The two countries had managed to circumvent the strict nuclear regime that forbids selling nuclear weapons but was silent about leasing a 'nuclear-propelled underwater stealth machine. The commissioning created an international furore.

The acquisition of the Project 670 Skat (NATO name- SSGN Charlie-I, wherein SS denotes "Submarine", G denotes "Guided Missile" and N denotes "Nuclear") cleared the decks for induction of another nuclear submarine nearly two decades later and a project to have a domestically-built nuclear submarine.

Powered by a single VM-4 type water-cooled nuclear reactor, Chakra had a submerged displacement of 5000 tons and could achieve a maximum speed of 24 knots. Indian and Russian authorities reiterate that Chakra was to be used strictly for training purposes, but it did create giant ripples in the Indian Ocean Region.

Chakra, literally translated as 'vortex or centre of psychic energy', was named after the Hindu god Lord Krishna's invincible weapon Sudarshana Chakra.

On 18th January 1988, Chakra embarked on a journey from Vladivostok to its new home, sailing through the frigid temperature of -15 degrees Celsius. During the journey, an emergency appendectomy was performed at a depth of 120m in the Pacific Ocean. VAdm Mihir K. Roy writes his book 'War in the Indian Ocean', "the routing was partly dived and partly on the surface via the South China Sea and Malacca Straits where she was escorted by an Indian frigate. She then dived in the Andaman Sea to arrive at Visakhapatnam on 2nd February 1988. The submarine was constantly tracked by the U.S and Australian Orion P3C aircraft."

On 3rd February 1988, the then Prime Minister Mr. Rajiv Gandhi, then Defence Minister Mr. K.C. Pant and their staff as well as then Indian Navy Chief Adm Nadkarni and the Flag Officer Commanding-in-Chief (East) VAdm S.C. Chopra got onboard Chakra for a short outing. Chakra also dived to give them a feel of the nuclear-powered submarine's potential and entered harbour in the evening to a rousing welcome by the naval fraternity and families of the crew and secured alongside berth 08, specially created for Chakra with attendant Radiation safety regime.

By this time, the navy had created a process of clearing a harbour for the berthing of nuclear vessels. This included survey by an Environmental Survey Committee (ESC) constituted by the Scientific Advisor to Defence Minister. A Radiation Safety Contingency Plan was also drawn up and implemented before the berthing of Chakra. Cmde A.V.R. Narayan Rao (later VAdm) was responsible for overseeing the creation of the entire infrastructure for Chakra in Visakhapatnam. His contribution is singularly significant.

There have been a lot of misgivings over the role of the Russian personnel onboard the submarine. There were 15 Russian Officers and 15 Senior Sailors (JCOs) who came to India for the lease period of three years. Out of these 30, only 7-8 personnel used to be on board as the vessel set on sail. Their role was to ensure that the lease conditions were complied with and that no reverse engineering on the reactor compartment and the missile equipment was undertaken in India. However, they had no responsibility whatsoever for the submarine operations. The Indian and Russian crew had spent time together since 1984 and were familiar with each other. During the sorties, the Russians would chat with the Indian crew or watch movies, read magazines etc.

Since the submarine was under Indian Naval command and control, the Indian crew had full and unfettered access to the whole sub. The reactor compartment usually is divided into two sections. The lower one is called the reactor space and is usually sealed and not visited, except when a fuel change is undertaken in a scheduled manner. The upper part is called the Reactor Equipment Space and is accessible only to crew personnel authorized by the Captain in writing. This entry and exit is controlled from the control room under the direct control of the Captain, mainly for adherence to Radiation Safety Practices.

Even the repairs and maintenance was undertaken by the Ship's crew and Naval Dockyard, Visakhapatnam (ND-V) personnel. There were a few Russian specialists stationed in Visakhapatnam on a requirement basis.

Although endurance sorties are of 6 weeks, the submarine used to be scheduled for 20 days at a time to train more personnel. In the third year, a 40 day sortie was carried out, which also involved the change of coast. The submarine did not enter any port and carried out exercises with the Eastern and Western Fleets. She surfaced only once off Goa to effect rendezvous with the aircraft carrier INS Viraat. As always, many technical and minor material problems did occur, which the crew resolved by themselves.

Captain (later RAdm) R.K. Sharma was in command, and Cdr (later Cmde) Arun kumar was the XO.

The Indian crew also conducted live underwater firing of the weapons, and the submarine participated in few exercises and the President's fleet Review in 1989.

The other area of misgivings is the return of the submarine. In November 1990, a commission of the Soviet GTD (General Technical Department) and GDE (General Engineering Department, which was later merged into Rosvoruzhenie, the state arms export company for new equipment, after 1992) had surveyed INS Chakra in Visakhapatnam and had recommended a lease extension by a year. But Admiral L. Ramdas on taking over as Chief of Naval Staff on 30th November 1990, decided not to take up that offer and directed the submarine to be returned to the Soviet Union. He was C-in-C (East) during the audit and had just shifted to Delhi as CNS. It is interesting to note that Adm Ramdas is currently known for his anti-nuclear activism.

VAdm Mihir has taken a different view of the transfer. Although the Soviet delegations had recommended the one-year extension, VAdm Mihir writes in his book 'War in the Indian Ocean,' "the demise of the Soviet Union coincided with the need for refuelling the Chakra which was almost at the end of her lease agreement".

The monetary cost of leasing the submarine may also be not the reason as the entire cost of the lease for a three-year lease was just Rs 54 Cr.

The submarine departed from Visakhapatnam on 15th December 1990 under the Indian Flag and command. The handing over took place on 04th

January 1991 in Vladivostok.

**Radiation issue:** The January/February 1990 issue of 'The Bulletin of Atomic Scientists' claimed that the Indian Navy might have received a second nuclear powered Charlie class from the Soviets as the first submarine it leased may have experienced radiation problems. Then in March, the same publication claimed that India had decided to cancel its plans to acquire six Soviet Charlie-I class. Radiation problems on the Charlie I, which it claimed is nicknamed "Chernobyl-class" in India, were more severe than reported in its previous Bulletin. The Bulletin quoted another publication, 'Navy News and Undersea Technology' (13 November 1989 edition), claiming that one Indian scientist may have died from radiation poisoning suffered on board the submarine. It further claimed that India is likely to return the two submarines already received from the Soviet Union.

Evidently, there was no second Charlie-I class on lease. On radiation deaths, the crew of the ex-Charlie-I class Chakra say that it cannot be answered with any veracity. Two officers, one the erstwhile Cdr (E) of the boat in the second year and one officer who was a reactor operator, died due to cancer in the last few years, more than a decade after returning the submarine. Whether there was any correlation has not been established. The crew wore personal dosimeters while onboard, and records used to be maintained with daily entries. It can only be a conjecture but cannot be stated with conviction. The pun 'Chernobyl class' has been described by the Chakra crew as 'utter garbage'.

# The Akula - II

As the navy was putting the Charlie-I class submarine through its phases, India and the Soviet Union began discussing the lease of a second submarine to India. However, when India returned the Charlie-I Class submarine in 1990 without extending the lease, the talks hit a pause. A need was felt to take a second nuclear submarine on the lease after the indigenous nuclear submarine, which was expected to be commissioned towards the end of lease of the Charlie-I Class, did not materialise.

In the meantime, India was heading for an economic crisis as it was experiencing Balance of Payment difficulties since 1985, and it came to a high point by 1991. In parallel, the Soviet Union displayed the symptoms of an impending collapse. India was hugely dependent on the Soviet Union for exports, diplomacy and import of critical items like weapons, industrial equipment etc. The countries traded on Rupee-Ruble terms. India began to diversify, and it found itself short of dollars as trade was not matured with the western countries.

In June 1991, Mr. P.V. Narasimha Rao, a reformist politician, was elected as the Prime Minister of the country. Along with Dr. Manmohan Singh as the finance minister, PM Rao unleashed very successful economic reforms. PM Rao is also credited with re-orienting India's diplomacy and engagement with the world.

In August 1991, the Indian defence minister Chandra Shekhar Singh visited Moscow, and among the topics he discussed was the reopening of talks for a lease of another nuclear submarine to India. It was not successful as the Soviet Union disintegrated in

December 1991. As the successor to the Soviet Union, Russia found it difficult to even supply spare parts for the conventional submarines it sold to India because of lack of capital and the production units became divided among the newly created states.

India and Russia began redefining their relations in 1993 to adjust to the post-cold war realities. Russian President Boris Yeltsin visited India in January 1993 and signed agreements for bilateral cooperation. The 1971 Indo-Soviet Treaty of Friendship and Cooperation was replaced with a new Treaty of Friendship and Cooperation. A defence cooperation agreement was signed to ensure continued availability of Russian arms, spare parts and joint production of military equipment. In May 1992, the contentious 1978 rupee-ruble trade agreement was replaced in favour of hard currency. PM Rao paid a reciprocal visit to Moscow in July 1994. Many declarations were signed, including the continuation of Russian military equipment exports to India. In December same year, eight more agreements were signed, including military and technical cooperation from 1995 to 2000.

The dissolution of the Soviet Union affected the schedule of discussions for almost a decade. Expertise gained through operating the Charlie-I was lost as another nuclear-powered vessel did not enter the Indian Navy's flotilla for the next two decades and the trained personnel had retired.

As the discussion for the possibility of leasing a nuclear submarine resumed, the navy expressed the view that it wanted a bigger sub so that it could train more personnel per sortie and for crew comfort.

A long term lease agreement is believed to have been signed during President Mr. Vladimir Putin's maiden visit to India in October 2000. Other important and relevant agreements signed during the visit were a Declaration on Strategic Partnership and an Inter-Governmental commission on military-technical co-operation co-chaired by the two countries' defence ministers.

Even though the negotiations were shrouded in utmost secrecy, the media world was buzzing with the news about the impending lease of another nuclear-powered attack submarine to India.

In the late 1990s and early 2000, open-source articles began stating that the two incomplete Project 971 Shchuka-B (NATO reporting name Akula) submarines Nerpa (Akula II) and Irbis (improved Akula I) were to be offered to India. In 2002 a Russian paper Novye Izvestia said India would lease two Project-971 nuclear-powered multi-role submarines (codenamed Bars in Russia and Shchuka-B in NATO classification), whose construction has been frozen for several years because of cash crunch. Under a contract negotiated by the Russian state arms exporter Rosoboronexport, India will fund their construction and acquire the submarines after five years. The plan was still to be approved by the Indian government, the paper said.

The submarines were touted as a balancing act against China's growing presence in the Indian Ocean and the Bay of Bengal until the Indian Navy inducts the indigenous nuclear-powered submarine - the Advance Technology Vessel (ATV).

In late 2004, the Russian news agencies began reporting the proposed lease of the Nerpa submarine for ten years to India under a 2004 secret deal. The contract was signed along with the INS Vikramaditya contract. The Indian version was expected to be armed with the 300-km Klub missiles. The Indian and the Russian officials denied those reports.

It is now known that the submarine deal was code-named as Project (I), and the delivery was expected in 2007.

In August 2005, a news website Bellona reported about the completion of International training center in Sosnovy Bor, 70 kilometers west of St. Petersburg in Russia, for training 300 Indian Navy personnel. It stated that the training was expected to begin by mid-September. The three sets of crew reportedly returned to India by 2007.

In June 2006, the RIA Novosti news agency quoted Russian Vice-Admiral Anatoly Shlemov stating that a nuclear-powered submarine which will reportedly be leased to India was launched at a shipyard in the Russian Far East. After undergoing sea trials, the Nerpa nuclear submarine was launched at the Amur shipyard and will join Russia's Pacific Fleet in 2007.

By the end of 2007, the Russian media stated that the final contract was signed during Indian Prime Minister Manmohan Singh's visit to Moscow in November 2007. This was supplementary to the 2004 main contract for the revised delivery schedule, which was delayed by nearly 18 months due to internal problems in Russia.

The deal hit a roadblock on 8th November 2008, when 20 personnel died inside the K-152 Nerpa due to the submarine's fire extinguishing system, which was reportedly activated without warning while the vessel was undergoing tests in the Sea of Japan. It was reported that the fire mishap delayed the taking over by the Indian crew, which had already assembled in Russia. An Indian delegation visited the submarine on 11th February 2009. A spat followed, and the Russians wowed to find money to retain the sub with the Russian Navy, and the submarine entered Russian naval service in December 2009.

In July 2011, the Russian Naval Chief Admiral Vladimir Vysotsky told Ria Novosti that the Russian built Nuclear Submarine is scheduled to be handed over to India by the year-end. "We will hand this submarine to the client by the year end…. The Indian crew is absolutely prepared for operating the submarine," he said.

On 20th August 2011, Interfax news agency quoted a source in Russia's military-industrial complex stating that the submarine had left the Russian Pacific coast for India "earlier this week." After the handover, an Indian crew had taken charge, and the submarine sailed crewed by a mixed Russian-Indian crew. In contradiction, RIA news agency stated that the crew was still training and the handover was not over.

On 30th December 2011, ITAR-TASS news agency quoted a senior Russian Navy official as saying, "The (handing over) signing ceremony happened on Thursday (29th December) at the Bolshoi Kamen ship building facility in the (Far East) Primorye region where the Nerpa is now based." "The submarine will depart for India in January (2012)," it added.

On 23rd January 2012, Rossiyskaya Gazeta (a Russian Government newspaper that publishes official decrees) stated that the submarine was rechristened as INS Chakra (S71). The ceremony was attended by the Indian ambassador to Russia, Mr. Ajai Malhotra.

RIA Novosti, on 21$^{st}$ February 2012, quoted a source in the Indian Defense Ministry stating, "We expect the submarine to arrive in India on March 30-31. The submarine is currently en route, bound for the port of Visakhapatnam."

Commanded by Captain P. Ashokan, Akula-II (rechristened as reincarnated INS Chakra (S1)) undertook a 40 days voyage, sailing underwater for the whole duration and covering more than 5,000 km from Vladivostok via Japan and South China Sea to reach home port Visakhapatnam on Saturday 31 March 2012. INS Ranjit escorted the submarine home.

On the occasion, Russian ambassador to India, Mr. Alexander Kadakin termed it "a shining example of the very confidential strategic cooperation between India and Russia."

INS Chakra - Akula II during Ex Tropex 2015

Affirming the game-changing dimension of INS Chakra's commissioning, the submarine's first skipper Captain P. Asokan said, "I commanded a conventional submarine before this, and we were restricted by battery power. But now, I have no restrictions. I can chase a vessel anywhere, overtake her, play games with her, and the nuclear plant never runs out of power."

Underlining the signal sent by the commissioning of Chakra, the then defence minister Mr. A.K. Antony said at the ceremony on 04$^{th}$ April 2012, "as peace and stability in the region (Indian Ocean Region) are crucial to peace in the world at large, it is imperative that the Indian Navy maintains a strong, stabilising and credible naval presence in the region."

At 12,000 ton displacement, INS Chakra is roughly four times the size of a conventional submarine. True to its name at origin, Akula (Shark), it is considered to be one of the deadliest submarines of its time.

The Soviet Union developed Akula II to counter the U.S's Los Angeles class SSNs. It is powered by a newly designed 190MW nuclear reactor. It has a fin mounted spherical escape sphere that is 20 feet wide and 50 feet tall; in case of an emergency, it can accommodate its entire 100-member crew and take them to safety.

The submarine is fitted with four 533mm torpedo tubes and four 650mm torpedo tubes. It is armed with the Russian Klub anti-ship missile and land-attack Klub 3m-14E missile.

The TEST-71MKE TV electric homing torpedo is already being used by the Indian Navy Kilo Submarines. The submarine can travel over 30 knots, dive up to a depth of 600 metres, and have noise levels next to zero.

The submarine crew wear a 'dosimeter' on the breast pocket of their overalls to measure radiation exposure. A radiation safety officer takes these readings on a specially rigged machine.

The JSC Amur Shipbuilding Plant is responsible for equipment, systems and product support for the Chakra. The responsibility of the support falls on Rosoboronservice (India) Ltd.

**Future**

In October 2013, PTI reported that India might finalise the deal for a second nuclear submarine lease to arrest the depleting fleet of submarines in the Indian Navy. The report came on the day of Prime Minister Mr. Manmohan Singh's visit to Russia. Quoting a 'highly placed government source', PTI stated that a proposal was approved by the Cabinet Committee on Security in its recent meeting headed by the prime minister. The deal is expected to cost India more than Rs. 6,000 crore.

Under the project, India is planning to finance the construction of the Akula Class submarine 'Irbis' in Russia, which could not be completed during the 1990s due to the lack of funds after the breakup of the erstwhile Soviet Union. The two countries have been holding negotiations in this regard for quite some time, and they were concluded recently. The construction of the submarine is expected to take at least three to four years.

In November 2013, the Defence Minister, Mr. Antony chaired the 13th meeting of the India-Russia Inter-Governmental Commission on Military-Technical Cooperation (IRIGC-MTC) with his Russian counterpart Mr. Sergey Shoigu. During the meeting, a prospective nuclear submarine lease from Russia to India was discussed.

India appears to have an interest in acquiring more SSGN's from Russia. On 12th December 2014, the Russian trade minister Mr. Denis Manturov said in an interview in New Delhi, "If India decides to have more contracts to lease nuclear submarines, we are ready to supply."

To place on record, some online Russian websites have indicated the availability of older Akula class submarines for the Indian Navy. These submarines can be refurbished and refitted for the Indian Navy use.

# INDIAN NUCLEAR SUBMARINE PROJECT - ATV – INS ARIHANT

*Without fanfare and recognition, our ballistic missile submarines patrolled the oceans of the Cold War in silent vigil, undetected and invulnerable, ready to strike, to deter our adversaries, and reassure our allies. And just as quietly, they set the standard for strategic deterrence and became the dominant leg of our strategic deterrent triad - our "ultimate insurance policy."*

**General Colin Powell**, US Army, chairman, Joint Chiefs of Staff

When it comes to submarines, secrecy is the operative word, and the story of the development of India's first domestically built nuclear military submarine is no different. Designed and developed under a project code-named Advanced Technology Vessel (ATV), the formal sanction for the programme was given by the then Prime Minister Indira Gandhi in 1983-84.

Since its inception, the existence of the nuclear-powered submarine programme has been a closely guarded secret. Despite the public launch of INS Arihant (S2) on 26$^{th}$ July 2009 by then Prime Minister's wife Gursharan Kaur, the submarine was kept under a wrap, and the Publicity Department of the Indian Ministry of Defence released only one carefully selected photograph of the lethal boomer.

Since the official launch, the ballistic missile-carrying submarine completed its harbour trials and began the sea trials in December 2014. The project has made India the first country outside the five permanent United Nations Security Council (UNSC)

members capable of constructing and operating such sophisticated platforms.

Aptly named the Arihant Class, the Destroyer/Slayer of Enemies, the submarines will be the final link in the Indian nuclear triad – the capacity to launch ballistic missiles from land, air and sea.

In sync with India's nuclear policy of "no first use", Arihant being an atomic submarine, can remain submerged undetected for longer than the conventional submarine, thus providing India with a survivable retaliatory strike if the country ever faces a nuclear strike.

The ATV Head Quarter was formally set up in 1983-84 with VAdm Mihir K. Roy as its first Director-General. The ATV HQ was purely to coordinate the development of design, equipment and the reactor for an indigenous nuclear-powered submarine. The DRDO manages the program with the support of the navy and BARC.

The ATV manages multiple organisations spread all over the country, the most important being the Ship Building Center (SBC) at Visakhapatnam and the training reactor at Kalpakkam. The ATV comes under the direct supervision of the Prime Minister's office to avoid bureaucratic delays. The Prime Minister of the day heads the ATV's apex committee. The project overcame many hurdles in technology denial and miniaturizing the nuclear reactor to fit the submarine. The ATV project was made successful by the close partnership of the DRDO, the Department of Atomic Energy (DAE) and other public and private sector undertakings. Private industrial players like Larsen and Toubro, and Tata Power helped in making the project a reality.

In an interview conducted with defence journalist Ritu Sharma a day after the launch of Arihant on 26$^{th}$ July 2009, VAdm Roy, who literally fathered the ATV project, said, "I said that I wanted to report directly to the Defence Minister, with no interference from secretaries and bureaucrats. It worked. Decisions were made across the table." The project was kept under the wraps lest it triggered an arms race on the Indian subcontinent. "We did not even have a name plate (outside the office). Nobody in my family, not even my wife, was aware what I was doing. On 26$^{th}$ July (when INS Arihant was launched) my grandchildren said: 'You never told us!'" he said.

With the satellites trying to trace the development of the nuclear attack submarine, precautions were also taken to cover the dry docks at the Ship Building Centre. "I got the dry docks covered; otherwise, satellites would have spotted the vessel and taken pictures," VAdm Roy added. The dry dock was constructed 50 meters below ground level.

VAdm Roy was also involved in back room negotiations with the then Soviet Union to garner their assistance for the project. "We were going fast (on the project). But there was a long delay. Then the USSR fell, and there were tremendous social, political and technological changes in the country. All contracts (on the ATV project) were changed. "In 2004, Russia stabilized, and we signed fresh contracts in dollars. Money was a problem for them because they (Russians) were short of dollars," VAdm Roy added.

**Steering the ATV**

VAdm Roy also provided an insight into the

organization in his article in 2010 naval Quarter Deck magazine. "The Director of Naval Design (Mr. S.) Paramanandhan and senior officers of the submarine arm such as Vice Admirals Shekhawat (later CNS) and Ravi Ganesh, later Commanding Officer of the first leased nuclear submarine INS Chakra, were part of the delegations for an integrated approach to submarine design and construction encompassing reactor technology, hull design, interfacing of weapons, periscope, masts, sonar and sensors.

"Hence considerable knowledge was augmented by setting up of Public-cum-Private partnership of PSUs such as BHEL, Midhani, NGEF, HEC, DRDL, BEL and DRDO laboratories along with the dynamic private sector industries of Larsen & Toubro, Walchandnagar, Tata and Kirloskar groups with their enormous resources. It is pertinent to state that India has over 200 universities and resource centers and IITs, with 7 million qualified workers providing resources for India's developing industries and other countries in Europe and the U.S.A.

"Group Captain Raghavan Gopalaswamy of DRDO was deputed to Harvard to assess management systems. On his return, he was held back at Visakhapatnam for discussions with Naval Dockyard and the Director-General of the Advanced Technology Vessel (ATV), VAdm Mihir Roy, who was also appointed as Secretary to the Government of India. The highly successful three-tier management structure was approved with the Prime Minister chairing the Apex Board, which all met regularly for quick decision making and implementation, which put the multi-technological project on a fast track."

## Hull Design

The initial ATV project began to construct a torpedo firing SSN. The definition of the project changed at a later date with the possibility of firing cruise missiles from torpedo tubes. It was further changed after India considered launching longer-range vertical launched cruise missiles. In May 1998, India conducted the Shakti Nuclear tests and declared the intention to build a sea-based deterrent. This prompted a change in design to accommodate ballistic missile tubes in the submarine. To fast track the construction the project was converted to a public-private partnership.

Arihant's design is based on Charlie-I class (Chakra) but has undergone incremental evolution as the Qualitative Requirements changed from an SSGN to an SSBN. It is clear that the Russians have not transferred any of their designs but have assisted and advised in formulating the design.

In mid-2000, Tehelka magazine published a report stating that Larsen & Toubro was awarded the contract to build the hull (code-named P 4102) at its Hazira dockyard facility in Gujarat and had already floated sections of it on a barge to Visakhapatnam.

The hull is said to be made of Russia sourced AB2 steel. L&T also won the outfitting contract.

An ex-employee of L&T recalls that the company also made the hull installed in the experimental reactor site at Kalpakkam. MDL did the outfitting.

The hull was mated with the experimental reactor in December 1987.

## Reactor Design

After the launch ceremony, the head of the ambitious project at the time of Arihant's launch

VAdm D.S.P. Verma (Retd), said that the vessel was ready and all the scientists needed was "to make its heart, the nuclear reactor, tick". The heart of Arihant – an 80 MW pressurized light water reactor – finally ticked or attained criticality in August 2013, after months of checking and rechecking all systems and subsystems of the boomer.

Like the hull design, the reactor design, too, has seen fundamental changes. It began as a Plutonium fuelled reactor and finally took shape as a Uranium run reactor. The Arihant reactor is fueled by 40% enriched Uranium. Light water is being used as the coolant and moderator. The Russian Charlie-1 Class had an 82 MW reactor.

A land-based prototype (PRP) of the Pressurised Water Reactor with 83 MW rating was first developed at Kalapakkam. It was mated with a section of the submarine's pressure hull. The Prototype reactor attained criticality on 11$^{th}$ November 2003 and was declared operational on 22$^{nd}$ September 2006. After three years of operations, the prototype yielded enough data to embark on constructing the production version of the reactor for the Arihant.

The 42 meters long PRP reactor has eight compartments housing complex electrical and control systems and simulating ocean conditions. Now, the prototype serves as a training centre for the nuclear submarine crew

After the launch, Arihant underwent an extensive trial with high-pressure steam in all its pipelines to check if all subsystems of its propulsion and power systems were working up to the mark. Harbour acceptance trial followed, which included flooding its ballast tanks and controlled dives to limited depths to conduct submergence tests. After the reactor went critical on 10th August, more shore-based tests were conducted to check the safety and robustness of the reactor. After that, on 13th December 2014, the submarine emerged from the Visakhapatnam harbour and sailed into the Bay of Bengal for extensive sea trials.

### Water Mist Fire Suppressant

INS Arihant features water mist fire suppressant instead of the Ozone-depleting Halons. The Centre for Fire, Environment & Explosive Safety (CFEES), a DRDO unit, has designed and tested a generation of water mist to fight pool fires. A water mist fire suppression system generates water droplets to sustain the fire sprinkler system with the help of nozzles.

The DRDO technology was validated for Arihant in a real scale 590 cubic meters cylindrical submarine fire simulation chamber. The simulation chamber was simulated as a nuclear submarine compartment having four decks.

The pool fire and spray fire with different heat release rates were created inside the chamber and suppressed with a water mist system with an internally mixed atomizer as a mist generator. The validation was successfully carried out as per IMO Circ 1165.

The technology has been accepted by the Indian Nuclear submarine programme, the Advanced Technology Vessel program (ATVP), for induction in S3 and S4 submarines as a replacement to Halons.

### Project 78 Underwater Missile Launcher

L&T has developed the P 78 underwater missile

launcher that simulates conditions to launch cruise and ballistic missiles vertically from a nuclear-powered submarine. P 78 is a large submersible barge with a control room large enough for around 8-10 operators to monitor the launch facility located at its centre (June 04, 2004, Deccan Herald).

The launcher was handed over to the DRDO in 2001. It has been used to test both Sagarika/K-15/BO5 and Brahmos anti-Ship Supersonic Cruise Missile.

Pantoon For Underwater Missile Tests

### Arihant's teeth - Sagarika/K-15/BO5

Sagarika/K-15/BO5 are names associated with the DRDO made underwater launched ballistic missile with a strike distance of approximately 700 Kms and a payload of 1000 Kg. During the sea trials of the Arihant, underwater test-firing of Sagarika from the vessel is also scheduled.

On 27th January 2013, the missile designated as

BO5 was tested from a pontoon from the Bay of Bengal off the coast of Visakhapatnam. It was the twelfth flight trial. The makers, the DRDO, stated that the radar monitored all the vehicle parameters all through the trajectory, and terminal events have taken place exactly as expected. The two-stage, solid fueled, 10 meter, six-ton SLBM will be integrated into Arihant. Arihant Class submarines are designed to carry twelve K-15 missiles capable of delivering nuclear warheads (Frontier India).

The same day, 'The Hindu' stated that the Submarine-Launched Ballistic Missile (SLBM) lifted off from a pontoon, rose to an altitude of 20 km and reached a distance of about 700 km as it splashed down in the waters of the Bay of Bengal near the pre-designated target point.

According to the then scientific advisor to Defence Minister V.K. Saraswat, the missile was tested for its full range of 700 km, and the mission met all its objectives. He said the impact accuracy of the medium-range strategic missile was in single digit.

The development of the missile is estimated to have begun in 1991-92.

### The Russian Involvement

On the day of the launch of the Arihant, Prime Minister Manmohan Singh thanked the Russians for their expertise and consultancy. The Soviet Union was considerably involved in the project during the beginning phases. Acknowledging their assistance, VAdm Mihir K. Roy told Ritu Sharma during the interview, "The submarine is built in India by Indians. We got a lot of assistance from them (Russians). Whenever we had a problem, we consulted them. We looked at drawings of Chakra. They have lot of respect for us. It (the submarine) has 70 per cent indigenous components."

Ex-Chief of India's Atomic Energy programme Anil Kakodkar also acknowledged the Russian role in the project during an interview published by "The Hindu" on August 16, 2009. Kakodkar, too admits that the Russians had consulted for the project. Below is the excerpt:

**Q: At Vizag, the Prime Minister went out of the way and thanked the Russians, and the Russian Ambassador was also present. What was the role of the Russians? India had leased a Russian nuclear submarine?**

**Kakodkar:** I would also like to thank our Russian colleagues. They have played a very important role as consultants; they have a lot of experience in this, so their consultancy has been of great help. I think we should acknowledge that.

**Q: Consultancy for what?**

**Kakodkar:** For various things, as you go along when you are doing things for the first time — with a consultant by your side, you can do it more confidently and these are difficult time-consuming challenges. So you have to do this without too much of iterative steps and consultancy helped in that.

**Q: So this** (Reactor) **is not a Russian design?**
**Kakodkar:** It is an Indian design.

**Q: Indian design, made in India, by Indians?**
**Kakodkar:** Yes, that's right.

In some past open-source reports, the naval officials have stated that the Russian involvement includes assistance in designing the vessel's reactor and guidelines in eventually mating it with the boat's hull.

### INS Arihant – A Technology Demonstrator or Limited Utility?

Is Arihant more of a technology Demonstrator than a deployable submarine? Officially acknowledging the existence of the Arihant project for the first time in December 2007, the then CNS Admiral Sureesh Mehta said, "It is a DRDO project and a technology demonstrator. It is somewhere near completion and will be in the water in two years."

INS Arihant at launch

On December 18, 2014, The Hindu quoted an ex-official involved with the program, stating that the Arihant will be of limited utility, "in effect it will be a limited utility submarine, if not just a technology demonstrator," said the source. Some key point stated by the official are listed below.

"The effective fuel inventory of the submarine

reactor is insufficient for longer duration deployment of the vessel far away from Indian shores, as it will necessitate frequent fuel changes that are time-consuming,"...Fuel change in a submarine reactor, he said, is a protracted and cumbersome process requiring the hull of the submarine to be cut open. The nuclear attack submarine (SSN) that India operates on a 10-year lease from Russia, INS Chakra (S1), for instance, is said to have reactor with a longer effective core life, granting it more time on patrol......The submarine arm of the Navy had previously expressed its reservations over the long "turnaround time" and frequent 'fuel change cycles, of the Arihant class of submarines."

The above has been refuted by ex-naval personnel who have served on the previous Charlie-I class and argued that the fuel life depends on the usage and is usually measured in KWH (Kilowat Hrs) at a specified time reactor load. If the navy were to run the reactor at full power, then the life would end at the designated KWH. In actuality, it would not be so. Therefore, a specified number of years cannot be laid down. If it meets all its trials successfully, it would be a deployable boat in its role.

As a lead submarine of the class, Arihant is the potential candidate for all tests, including mating with missiles and midlife refuelling. The other activities will include repairing the propulsion plant, restoring the submarine to an operational state after modernising sensors and weapons etc. Learnings will be passed to faster turnaround of the subsequent submarines. Being the lead submarine, there will be teething problems, which would be overcome as she goes along. However, as a second Strike option, she would fulfil her role.

## Arihant's Technical and Tactical Data

The 6000-tonne submarine is powered by an 80-megawatt capacity nuclear reactor and can acquire surface speeds of 22 to 28 kmph (12-15 knots) and submerged speed up to 44 kmph (24 knots). It will be carrying a crew of 95 men and will be armed with torpedoes and 12 ballistic missiles.

Arihant is 111 meters long, 11 meters broad, and 15 meters tall. The head of the submarine is fitted with sonar. There is a living room just after the sonar, followed by a space that will hold the torpedoes and land-attack cruise missiles, followed by a Control Room, a Periscope, Galley, Missile Tubes, Nuclear Reactor, Turbine, Electric Motor and Propeller shaft.

## Post Arihant its INS Aridaman

Even as the defence authorities refrain from acknowledging the construction of follow up nuclear attack submarines after Arihant, the open sources quote officials saying that with Arihant being more of a technology demonstrator, the knowledge gained in constructing the underwater vessel will help in faster construction of the next in line.

On the sidelines of the launch of Arihant, its programme director VAdm (Retd) D.S.P Verma said, "This is the first time that such a project (construction of a nuclear submarine) was conceived and undertaken in the country…. All the facilities and the infrastructure had to be set up from the scratch…. The second submarine will have more indigenous components." He did not elaborate any further.

Echoing the same sentiments VAdm Mihir K. Roy added, "The first one is always a technological demonstration. But we will have a series of it. The second submarine will be ready and will take lesser time."

On 14$^{th}$ January 2012, The Hindu reported the construction of a second submarine of the same class. Informed sources told the paper that the construction of a second Arihant-class nuclear submarine, to be named INS Aridaman, is moving fast at the Shipbuilding Centre (SBC) in Visakhapatnam. "The boat, under outfitting now, is headed for a year-end launch. Meanwhile, hull fabrication is on for the third Arihant-class nuclear-powered ballistic missile submarine," the sources said.

Aridaman was again in the news on March 8, 2014, when the Express News Service reported an accident on the Aridaman project, killing one worker and injuring two others. The accident, sources said, took place when the hull was being pressure tested, and one of the hatches flew apart.

Frontier India's article on the water mist fire suppression system also confirms the existence of third submarine of the class, "The technology for Water Mist Fire Suppressant has been accepted by Indian Nuclear submarine program, the Advanced Technology Vessel program (ATVP), for induction in S3 and S4 submarines as a replacement to Halons." The article is based on a report in a DRDO publication. The existence of S4 has also been reported by a company Polyphase Motors, which mentions in a trade website that it has supplied more than 340 Nos. motors for Arihant and Successors- S3 and S4.

On 15th October 2014, Zee news reported, "India plans to a few submarines of the Arihant class, and two or three more are reportedly under construction already."

The navy has followed the same predictable logic of having a minimum of one submarine in operational roles while others go for refits, repairs and replenishments with three SSBNs.

It is understood that the Aridaman is bigger in size compared to Arihant to enable it to operate with double the number of missiles being carried by Arihant.

The name Aridaman is a Sanskrit word that means destroyer of the enemies. The author speculates that the name of the third Arihant class SSBN 'S4" could be Amitrasudan which also means destroyer of the enemies.

Joseph P. Chacko

# THE UNTOLD STORY OF THE ARIHANT-THE VANQUISHER OF ENEMIES !

In August 2013, just before India's Independence Day celebrations, Prime Minister Manmohan Singh congratulated the team that made the nuclear submarine INS Arihant's nuclear reactor go critical at Visakhapatnam, appropriately calling it a giant step for India's security with the words, "I am delighted to learn that the nuclear propulsion reactor on board INS Arihant, India's first indigenous nuclear powered submarine, has now achieved criticality. I extend my congratulations to all those associated with this important milestone, particularly the Department of Atomic Energy (DAE), the Indian Navy and the Defence Research and Development Organisation (DRDO). Today's development represents a giant stride in the progress of our indigenous technological capabilities. It is a testimony to the ability of our scientists, technologists and defence personnel to work together for mastering complex technologies in the service of our nation's security."

This seminal achievement got eclipsed by the media coverage of the reverberations of the unfortunate explosion and sinking of the Kilo-class submarine INS Sindhurakshak with eighteen deaths in the Naval Dockyard at Mumbai four days later on 14th August night. Submarine operations call for high safety standards and quality control checks, as failure of a small system, component, or pump can cause high costs and damages. Each crew member has to be an all-round professional, and physiologically suited for underwater service and hardships, especially in nuclear submarines. In America, Admiral Hyman D. Rickover known as the father of nuclear submarines, interviewed every officer and sailor personally for service in nuclear boats, and even rejected Lt Cdr Elmo Zumwalt Jr (Bud), who later went on to become US Navy's (USN) 19th and youngest Chief of Naval Operations (CNO).

The Sri Lankan underwater explorer, inventor and fiction writer Sir Arthur Clark once said, "Any sufficiently advanced technology is indistinguishable from magic." The statement well applies to miniature nuclear reactors on submarines, which enables men and now women in submarines to safely and comfortably live and operate underwater for months before the submarine surfaces. Oxygen is regenerated under water from sea water. The advantage of a nuclear submarine over conventional submarines is, she can propel under water for months as long as the food lasts. In American submarines, the record is three months, and U.S.N appoints two crews, gold and blue, to man and maintain the sub alternately. A nuclear submarine is 'Pearl' shaped, and therefore has faster speed under water than on the surface. Inertial navigation gadgets, underwater receivers and sonars, ensure her safe navigation and communications.

Coded signals to launch missiles or weapons can be sent to the submarine from the nation's political nuclear command authority, or through National Security Agency (NSA) as in India extracted from the Prime Minister's black attaché case of codes, held also by the submarine. The low frequencies signals are received (as in India's case Very Low Frequency

(VLF) from INS Kattabomman) while submerged by trailing an antenna, and now Blue Green lasers that can penetrate the sea. In America, the President's code box is called 'Football'. No nation can afford to be dependent on another nation for its nuclear submarine reactors, which form the vital component of the strategic assets of a nation for nuclear security and deterrence from the sea.

It is to the credit of the Indian Navy planners that they realised this and joined hands with scientists at BARC as early as the 1980's when naval officers were deputed to the BARC's Atomic Training Centre and jointly began designing miniature nuclear reactors in a classified group code-named the new 'New Reactor Projects Division' which was carved out of the existing BARC's Reactor Engineering Division, with dozens of engineers as the 'core' design team. It had the blessings of DAE Chairman Dr. H.N. Sethna, and Dr. Raja Ramanna Director BARC called the "Father of the Indian nuclear programme" for the 1974 nuclear blasts.

The team included Messrs Mehra, Grover, Yadav, and S. Basu, the current head of BARC, under a brilliant US and France trained atomic scientist Anil K. Anand. In his personal autobiography 'Second Strike', Anand has included some details of the work by the 'New Reactor Projects Division' and he was a colleague of Dr. Anil Kakodkar at BARC. He studied zircaloy joints and tubes and calandria ends in France's Pressure Water Reactors (PWR) at the Commissariat à l'Énergie Atomique at Scalay near Paris in Section des Advances, for the French EL-4 PWR reactor at Brennilis and brought back the techniques which were to help him at BARC for

PWR reactors which he says was late Dr. Homi Bhabha's dream. Late Dr. Vikram Sarabhai interviewed Anand for the BARC job, and he recalls meeting Dr. Bhabha. All this later helped the naval nuclear submarine reactor project.

Anand in 'Second Strike' relates details of his torrid love affair in France with an affluent divorcee medical doctor he calls Ma Dame (Meera), who was also there for training from Thailand on scholarship and they lived together in the same Hotel in romantic Paris. Later he married her, though many years his senior. The team under Anand from BARC went on to design and build the training half submarine with a miniature reactor (S1) at IGCAR at Kalpakkam, which went critical on 11th November 2003 and operational on 22nd September 2006. It's replica is the Arihant's pressured Uranium U-235 light water reactor.

The challenge ashore was to make a dynamo meter to absorb the power which is used in a submarine to power the propeller. No nation readily shares these details and nuclear technologies. Anand engineered the fuel rods and pellets for the reactor and cladding from imported Uranium (from Russia) and Indian oxides. Marine reactors are peaceful nuclear facilities, and outside IAEA safe guards.

The over Rs 8,000 crore Advanced Technology Vehicle ( ATV) classified project as it was dubbed in 1983, was initiated by late Dr. Raja Ramanna ( PhD in Western music and PhD in Atomic science both from UK) with Prime Minister Mrs. Indira's blessings as both BARC and Department Of Atomic Energy (DAE) were under PMO. The veil of secrecy placed on project for many years was lifted on 26th July

2009, when Mrs. Gursharan Kaur wife of Prime Minster Dr. Manmohan Singh, in his presence, ceremoniously unveiled the submarine to the media and invited guests at the Ship Building Centre (SBC) Visakhapatnam, by breaking the customary coconut to name and bless all those who sail in her. Arihant was floated out of the dry dock and berthed alongside. No photography or visit to the 6000-ton black menacing hull was allowed. In his speech, Dr. Manmohan Singh thanked all those who had contributed to the project, including the Russian technicians in the presence of the Russian Ambassador Alexander Kadakin, in what is considered the acme of nuclear technology master light water miniature uranium reactors in confined submarine spaces. Only U.S.A, Russia, France, China and UK, with U.S help, have mastered the technology and have the capability to engineer and manufacture the submarine, reactor and fit underwater launched nuclear-tipped missiles.

Anand reveals that the Arihant with the BARC reactor was assembled and outfitted at SBC with indigenous and imported equipment in a unique Public-Private Partnership (PPP) between BARC, the Navy and DRDO with engineering giant L&T, in a leased shed and dry dock in the segregated part of the large Naval Dockyard Visakhapatnam. The naval dockyard at Visakhapatnam was also built with Soviet help in the 1970s with CNS Admiral Sergey Gorshkov's support, when India's largest cargo-handling port was not so congested, as it is today. Gorshkov saw the future congestion and the narrow channel as unsuitable, and advised against the site, and offered to build a green-field naval dockyard at

Bimlipatam, but PM Mrs. Gandhi did not agree, fearing Soviets would demand basing facilities at the height of the Cold War. The Navy is now rushing to build a new green field submarine base South of Gangavaram dubbed Varsha as Visakhapatnam is congested and has a narrow channel that can be blocked in these days of terrorism.

Arihant was berthed alongside at the SBC at Visakhapatnam and underwent rigorous reactor safety checks and harbour trials. The submarine houses the computer-controlled and home-built reactor installed by BARC and industry, which produces steam under pressure to run the single multiple bladed propeller and generators to power equipment from inside the sealed nuclear pressure vessel. The reactor began operations at low power since the power cannot be utilized (propulsion, Turbo Alternator's (TA) and other ship's load), which at sea is done by equipment at action stations (on deployment). Usually, in the harbour, the reactor is operated at the TA regime and is at about 30%.

Soviet technicians and Indo-Soviet Working Groups helped the programme as the ATV's consultants at SBC and for design checks in Russia provided by the navy. An Indian naval submarine design group (SDG) was set up under the Indian Institute of Technology (IIT), and Greenwich trained naval architect, Cdr Raj Chaudhary with experience of Royal Naval College in Greenwich and HDW design, who worked closely with late engineering officer Cdr Gurmeet Singh, the first naval graduate of the BARC Training School, both later Rear Admirals with long service in ATV. The duo and BARC's Anand as the project director of the training reactor, executed all the planning and later execution of the setting up of the training submarine and nuclear reactor at Indira Gandhi Atomic Research Centre (IGARC) at Kalpakkam, South of Chennai. It is like the Royal Navy's smaller training reactor Jason at Greenwich, on which the author was exposed twice in 1974 while pursuing the Staff College in London.

Initially, MOD and MDL wanted to build the ATV training submarine facilities at MDL's Greenfield Mangalore site, but it is to the credit of the naval planners, and BARC who wished to bring in L&T who convinced MOD to decide against Mangalore, as nuclear facilities with expertise were available at Kalpakkam and visits to submarines and the naval dockyard at Visakhapatnam feasible, which had mastered the medium refit of Foxtrot class submarines from 1641K documents when INS Khanderi cleared all trials to the surprise of the Soviets. Bharat Heavy Plates & Vessels, BHEL Trichy, ECIL and BEL close by were involved.

Adm Gorshkov is credited for getting Soviet Union's leadership to lease the nuclear submarine INS Chakra in 1987, reposing faith that Indian Navy officers and sailors could rise to the challenges of operating nuclear submarines, and a lot of experience was gained in the running of nuclear submarines safely. The entire project was under the stewardship of the Prime Minister's Office (PMO), the Scientific Adviser to the Minister of Defence (SA/MOD) and DRDO head, with naval Project Directors with autonomous powers. The PDs and later DG of the ATV projects were Vice Admirals late MK (Mickey) Roy, an illustrious French-trained Alize Observer from 1984 who was also Dr. Ramanna's friend and paying guest roommate in London, followed by Bharat Bhushan, the UK trained engineering specialist, R.N. Ganesh, the first Captain of INS Chakra, trained at Vladivostok, Pramod Bhasin a missile specialist electrical officer who had served in Britain and the Soviet Union and prepared the Styx P-20 missiles for the 1971 war, D.S.P Verma and currently S. Prabhakar.

Bhasin courageously cut steel as Project Director in 1999 on his birthday with CNS Admiral Vishnu Bhagwat's support, who took great interest and visited the project. Unfortunately, Bhagwat soured his relations with the government and even demanded an audit of the ATV project and was unceremoniously sacked on 31st December 1998.

After the DRDO confirmed Airhant's clearing final harbour trials and safety checks, on 15th December 2014, Arihant proceeded to sea for the challenging 'first of class' sea and deep-diving trials. Later Arihant will install the 'Plug & Play' K-15/B-05 Sagarika vertical launch 750 km nuclear-tipped missiles to join India's Triad for India's nuclear deterrence.

On BARC's Foundation Day in 2014, an illustrated PowerPoint presentation was made by Dr. Anil Anand, who also headed the Propulsion Reactor Project (PRP1) at Kalpakkam as its Director since 1984 till his retirement in 2000. PRP-1 was the nickname for the prototype training reactor with a half submarine hull with all machinery set up at IGARC at Kalpakkam, which successfully went critical on 11th November 2003 and operational on 22nd December 2006 with high power. PRP 1 and has been training the navy's nuclear submarine key crews and now runs like a naval establishment, with a wardroom and accommodation at IGARC at Kalpakkam under INS Adyar's administration from Chennai.

It is the PRP1 that gave confidence to the ATV project staff to test and insert the operational reactor in Arihant and proves Indian scientists can make submarine reactors and the fuel pellets and also teach the naval crew how to operate it with all the safety checks. Dr. S. Basu, the current Director of BARC, was the No 2 of the PRP project. It is pertinent to record that USS Nautilus took 16 years from 1944 when it was authorized to 1955 for sea trials and 1960 to join the fleet, while Russia took 16 years to build its first, second-generation SSN -093 submarine (1990-2006). The Arihant achievement must be judged and be lauded.

By **CMDE Ranjit B. Rai** (Retd.)

Marker boom for the propeller of a SSK or the Kilo since the Prop is submerged some distance aft of the visible part of the aft casing. This is to warn other vessels so that they do not come close to it. Image: Joseph P. Chacko

Joseph P. Chacko

# THE INDIGENOUS SSGN'S

Naval planners often see SSN's as invulnerable sea denial assets, which can complicate or deter or prevent a superior force from exploiting control of the sea.

In the 1950s, the Indian naval planners began looking at SSNs to establish a presence as far away as Indonesian and Chinese waters. The presence of the U.S in the Indian Ocean was a stronger motivation for the SSN programme. (Thomas, R. G. C., in The politics of Indian naval rearmament, 1962-74, Pacific community, Apr. 1975)

By the end of 1960s, India began operating the Foxtrot class to gain the experience of operating submarines. Simultaneously the studies started to design and build a nuclear propulsion for propelling future submarines. By 1984, India began preparations to build a nuclear submarine under the project ATV as described in the previous chapter. The intention was to construct a total of 6 SSN's.

Around that time, some observers had speculated that India would attempt to buy or lease as many as eight SSN's (Eric Arnett, Military Technology: the case of India, SIPRI Year Book 1994)

Due to the lack of experience in building a submarine, India tried unsuccessfully to ink a deal with Sweden for technology transfer and construction of submarines in India. Later, India sealed a deal for the construction of HDW Type 1500 submarines in India. The project was delayed and then closed after bribery charges and cost escalations.

In the meantime, the Soviet Union offered to help India build the nuclear submarines and loaned a

Charlie-I class for training. The indigenous submarine failed to materialise even after the end of the lease.

By the time the design for the torpedo firing nuclear submarine changed to cruise missile firing SSGN.

After 1998 nuclear tests, the priorities shifted to 'no first use' and 'nuclear triad', and the design of the submarine changed to accommodate a VLS for ballistic missile firing. The navy began developing an SSBN for the undersea nuclear deterrent. The navy found the conventional attack submarines good enough for deployment in the nearby Arabian Sea, the Bay of Bengal and even at the choke points at Malacca Straits. The SSN's which could loiter throughout the Indian Ocean and beyond at discretion, began getting a lesser priority.

Although the HDW SSK project learnings were lost after almost a decade of idle capacity, India's quest for technology acquisition continued. In 2005 India signed a deal for indigenous construction of Scorpene submarines. The Scorpene submarines use Type 80 HLES high-yield steel for pressure hull, the same as used for the French Navy's nuclear submarines. The design reportedly allows for the installation of a small nuclear reactor. However, the claim is disputed by the naval personnel who have been involved with the project. The diameter of the pressure hull of the Scorpene is 6.2 m, which is not enough to house even a mini reactor. The minimum diameter of a pressure hull for that is about 7.1m.

One of the interesting aspects of the Scorpene submarine is that all equipment, systems, pipes and valves fitted are tested to nuclear submarine standards at the DCNS facility at Cherbourg, France. Particular attention has been given to noise reduction during fitment. The Scorpene machinery is mounted on a raft with shock absorbers which helps in dampening the noise. An extra tight turn or a bend in the pipe and the consequent effect on noise are studied in detail. The testing also ensures a large MTBF or mean time between failures. Indian entities have acquired a range of technologies and processes during the construction phase, and the navy plans to use them in future submarine projects.

In February 2015, the Indian government approved the construction of 6 SSN's. In view of the approval, the delayed 30-year submarine construction plan has been tweaked and will retain 18 SSK's instead of 24.

Little is known about the design of the 6 SSN's. In the past, western analysts have tried to correlate the repair of two Indian diesel-powered Kilo-class submarines at Severny machine-building plant in Severodvinsk with the acquisition of technical design for a nuclear sub. The same plant has built the Russian fourth-generation Yasen-class SSN 'Severodvinsk' designed by Rubin design office. Rubin is the design house for the Kilo-class submarines too. Based on the Akula Class, which India currently operates, Severodvinsk deploys VLS capable of launching anti-ship and anti-land cruise missiles. This is not factual as the repair of Kilos was done by Zvezdochka State Machine Building Enterprise.

The media states that the Naval Staff Qualitative Requirements (NSQR) is yet to be decided but has quoted the tonnage of about 6000 tons. However, the officials familiar with the project estimate the SSGN to be between 2500 – 4500 tons.

The first SSN will not fructify for the next 10 years as the NSQR is expected to firm up in two years, then there is an estimated seven years gestation period and one year for testing. India is scheduled to field two aircraft carriers even before the first SSN takes shape. A Carrier Battle Group (CBG) requires a minimum of one SSN for its protection.

India has already leased INS Chakra and requires two more SSN's to cater to the 2 CBG's. Talks for the lease of one more SSN is underway. So India may have approached Russia for one more SSN. This also might explain comments by the Russian trade minister Mr. Denis Manturov on the 12th December 2014, that if India decides to have more contracts to lease nuclear submarines, Russians were ready to supply.

# P-75 (INDIA)

The navy's Project 75 (India) or (P-75 (I)) is the second line of six submarines envisaged in the 30-year submarine building plan. In 2009 the navy sought RFI from global vendors for six Project 75(I) class submarines independent of the 2005 Scorpene contract.

The Defence Acquisition Council gave the clearance to the project on 25$^{th}$ October 2014. The P 75 (I) submarines are expected to be bigger than the Scorpene-class and now require a fit of AIP. All the subs are to be built in India.

The P 75 (I) has been in the news for over a decade and with multiple versions. The first version was Amur 1650 being built at Hindustan Shipyard Limited since Mazagon Dock Limited (MDL) was expected to be awarded the Project 75 Scorpene project. The initial approval for this project was given in the CCS approval of the 30 Year plan and was to be of an Eastern Design (Russian) during Phase 1 of the plan. All negotiations with the Russians were finalized by December 2001, including TOT aspects. Due to a delay in the signing of the Scorpene contract, the P75(I) was held back. The Union Government changed in May 2004, and the project was put on the back burner. Subsequently, in 2006, the QRs were amended to include the AIP. There was no question of a Western Design in P 75(I) because as per the CCS approval of the 30-year plan there were to be two diverse sources for the design and equipment.

The second version was an enlarged Scorpene since Indians would have already picked up submarine building skills from the P-75 project, and India has options for four more Scorpene submarines. The French have already offered a Super Scorpene for the P-75 (I) project. India Today, on 06th December 2010, reported, "France will offer India a bigger version of its Scorpene conventional diesel-electric (SSK) submarine for a $5 billion (Rs.30,000 crore) contract for six submarines. This is the world's largest order for conventional submarines."

Stating this, Patrick Boissier, Chairman and CEO of French shipbuilder DCNS, confirmed that the design of the existing Scorpene submarine could be lengthened with the addition of more sections, including AIP."

Another gossip is that the French might offer the 4,750-ton SMX Ocean concept design based on the basic Barracuda (the French SSN) layout, masts, and combat system. The Barracuda SSN model was displayed at Defexpo India 2014.

The third version was building an Indian design copied from Advanced Technology Vessel (ATV). This was denied by the navy and was probably true for the indigenous SSGN project.

The fourth version was an open tender. The speculated Submarine contenders included France's DCNS with Scorpene, Russia's Rubin Amur 1650, German HDW Type 214, Spain's Navantia S-80, Sweden's Kockums Archer-class and proposed Italian-Russian S1000 platform.

The fifth version is that the submarine is from the East. The speculation began after the visit of a Rosoboronexport team in 2014 to hold discussions for the sale or lease of two Amur-class submarines to help restock the shrinking force. This could also influence the P 75 (I) tender.

A tender is definite, and the possible contenders have indicated that they are willing to integrate vertical tubes for firing Brahmos Cruise Missile. Russia's Central Design Bureau for Marine Engineering Rubin has pitched with Amur 1650. Rubin's Amur 950 model already features 10 Vertical launch Tubes. DCNS has offered to build more Scorpene submarines since India is already producing these submarines. HDW has confirmed that it will participate in the P 75 (I) tender. "We are going to submit the Type 214 for Project 75(I) with air-independent propulsion (AIP). We have already delivered 15 of these, so Type 214 is proven," said a ThyssenKrupp Marine Systems spokesman to Sheperd Media on 9 February 2014. Spanish Navantia S-80 is another contender. Navantia is already involved in transferring technology for the Scorpene project and has replied to the RFI.

On 18th January 2015, the Hindustan Shipyard Limited (HSL) inked a memorandum of understanding with South Korea's Hyundai Heavy Industries Co Limited for participation in the P-75(I) project. The news comes after HSL formed a consortium with BHEL (Bharat Heavy Electricals Limited) and Mishra Dhatu Nigam Limited (MIDHANI) for the project.

There is a possibility of Japanese participation in the tender. The Times of India on 29th January 2015 published a piece of news stating that the government had asked the Japanese government whether it would be interested in the over Rs 50,000 Crore project. A source told the newspaper, "With Japan recently ending its decades old self-imposed arms export embargo, New Delhi has forwarded "a proposal" to Tokyo to "consider the possibility" of making its latest diesel-electric Soryu-class submarines in India.... If Japan is really interested, it will have to form a joint venture with an Indian public/private shipyard." The paper further stated, "But the 4,200-tonne Soryu submarines, manufactured by Mitsubishi Heavy Industries and Kawasaki Heavy Industries, may not meet Indian requirements. Japan will also be just one of the contenders for the mega programme, called Project-75-India if it agrees to throw its hat into the ring." The Soryu submarines are already equipped with AIP, and the new batch of 6 Soryus for the Japanese Navy (JMSDF) is planned to be built around the Lithium-ion batteries."

A Defence Acquisition Council meeting in 2014 had directed the MoD to set up a committee to identify shipyards in India capable of building submarines. The committee headed by the navy's Controller of Warship Production and Acquisition VADM A.V. Subhedar along with representatives from the Navy and MoD conducted a survey of shipyards along both the coasts, including the Garden Reach Ship-Builders, Hindustan Shipyard, Goa Shipyard, L&T, Mazgaon Docks, ABG Shipyard and Pipavav Shipyard.

During the undocking event of the first P 75 project submarine on $6^{th}$ April 2015, the Defence Minister praised the MDL for being the only shipyard in India with the country with submarine building experience and wondered if the private yards could jointly build the P-75I project submarines with MDL.

**P-75 (I) and Brahmos integration**

Integration of Brahmos anti-ship cruise missile with the P 75 (I) project was not on the cards during the approval of the 1999 Submarine Building program. In 2014 the prospective bidders indicated that they are willing to integrate Brahmos in their design. When the Brahmos Missile took off vertically from the submerged platform on 20$^{th}$ March 2013, the then CEO & MD of BrahMos Aerospace Dr. A. Sivathanu Pillai said "BRAHMOS missile is fully ready for fitment in P75 (I) of the Indian navy in vertical launch configuration which will make the platform one of the most powerful weapon platform in the World."

However, officials involved in the past with the project argue that the Brahmos integration was not mentioned in the last RFI.

The Navy is seeking new submarines with both land-attack missile capabilities and AIP. There is a possibility that the P-75 (I) may not feature a VLS for launching the Brahmos missile because BrahMos Aerospace has indicated the creation of a tube-launched 'Brahmos Mini' version of the missile.

# SUBMARINES – THE DEBATES WITHIN

*"No matter how many tradeoffs we study of other ways to spend the money we need to pay for nuclear propulsion, we will always be faced with comparing unlike things; none of the tradeoffs accord freedom from logistic support for propulsion fuel which is provided by nuclear propulsion. The other tradeoffs provide additional defense protection to the CVAN [nuclear aircraft carrier], but none of them increase the offensive capability of the CVAN as well - as does nuclear propulsion in the escorts. To compare a larger number of conventional escorts with a smaller number of nuclear escorts at equal cost is not to compare alternative ways of achieving the same capability; it is merely to compare two different capabilities that can be achieved with the same amount of money."*
**Adm Hyman George Rickover** (Retd), USN

The efficacy of the submarine as an offensive weapon of war was truly established in WW II. Although the U boats had shown their usefulness in WW I, but they were vulnerable as most of the time the boats were on the surface and dived only to carry out torpedo attacks. In a true sense, they were more of submersibles. Though the Snorkel on submarines came about only at the end of WW II and could not be used to establish its significance, but the very large scale destruction of allied shipping effected by the U boats, almost bringing the allied forces to their knees, underlined the importance of the submarine as a very potent offensive weapon. It was the evolution of the Convoy system and the air anti-submarine warfare (AASW) that changed the tide after 1943. The focused development of Anti-Submarine Warfare(ASW) measures during the war, such as ASDICs or presently termed SONAR also played a significant part in defeating the German Submarine campaign. The Pacific U.S Navy Submarine campaign also played a decisive part in defeating the Imperial Japanese Navy. Consequently, the potential of the importance of the submarine as a potent offensive weapon of war was firmly established.

Similarly, the evolution of a Carrier Task Force (CTF) later to evolve as Carrier Battle Group (CVBG) also took place just prior to and during the WW II. The dramatic attack by the Japanese Carrier Task Force, known as Kido Butai, on Pearl Harbour, in which a group of carriers with other escorts almost succeeded in wiping out the US Pacific Fleet, highlighted the immense potential of naval carrier based aviation. Ever since, there has been a debate of sorts on submarine versus the carrier as the focus of maritime warfare.

Tremendous efforts and resources, in research and development on enhancing the capabilities of both these aspects of naval warfare were put into place after the WW II. Great strides were made in developing ASW in which a CVBG was to play a great role as well as in developing a true submarine.

In the Submarine sphere, the efforts resulted in the emergence of a nuclear powered submarine, which could be termed as a true submarine as it would be totally independent of the atmosphere and unlimited in its endurance except for that of the crew. In parallel, techniques to reduce noise and other signatures of the submarine were developed. This increased the gap between the submarine and ASW forces as the vagaries of the medium in which the submarine operates, limited the extent of development in ASW. Ways were found to increase the endurance of the conventional submarines and the use of Snorkel played a significant part in enlarging the radius of operation and endurance of the conventional submarines, but this still did not do away with the requirement to periodically surface to periscope depth (PD) to charge batteries and to change the air inside the boat. It is at such times that the boat is most vulnerable to detection by surface and air surveillance. The more recent development of Air Independent Propulsion (AIP) system is a move to resolve this handicap. However, AIP is also limited in its capability, in that it cannot provide speeds more than 2-3 knots. Requirement of a submarine to manoeuver at higher speeds in an offensive mission close to enemy waters is essential in its operational profile. Silencing techniques on nuclear powered submarines further enhanced their effectiveness. The Cold War defined a new strategic role for the nuclear powered submarine wherein the nuclear powered submarines equipped with ballistic missiles (SSBNs) came into being. These boats were capable of delivering their warheads from the safe confines of own harbours and gave a second strike capability in a Nuclear conflict. The limitless endurance and speed of the nuclear powered boats also gave them the freedom to approach and attack a surface force from any direction. The development of sub surface launched cruise missiles added another lethal dimension to the submarines, both nuclear powered and conventional, which increased the strike range of the submarine, thereby bringing greater area of influence under its ambit of operations. This gave birth to nuclear powered boats with cruise missiles (SSGNs) and conventional boats with cruise missiles (SSGs). Further, the silencing techniques on Nuclear powered boats and the speed to keep up with a surface force also enabled such a boat (SSN) to perform ASW role either independently or as a part of a CVBG. These developments, which gave multiplicity of roles to the submarine, offered versatility in exploitation of the submarine in maritime operations. Thus the nuclear powered boats as well as the conventional boats came to occupy a pre-eminent position in the matrix of maritime calculations. Many believed that with such boats the gravity of maritime warfare had shifted heavily in favour of the submarine. These capabilities and developments also enabled the submarine to graduate from a platform of sea denial to sea control.

On the other end of the spectrum, great advances were made in Carrier based aviation operations as well. The methods of launch and recovery of aircraft became more sophisticated enabling speedy operations and enhanced endurance of Carrier based aircrafts. Evolution of design and propulsion systems, including nuclear, enabled larger aircraft carriers to be made thereby positioning greater number of aircraft capable of performing a variety of roles such as air early warning (AEW), ASW, ordnance delivery, fighter interceptors for air defence etc. Shipborne helicopter operations from frigates and destroyers added to the ASW capabilities of a CVBG. Thus evolved the concept of mutual protection against anti surface (ASU), anti-submarine (ASW) and anti-air (AA) of a CVBG vis a vis the Aircraft carrier and its escorts. This nailed the argument against a CVBG that an aircraft carrier is an expensive option in maritime warfare, as it requires too many escorts for its safety and protection and that these assets could be better used in independent operations.

In the entire debate it is necessary to understand the concepts of Sea control, Sea denial and Power projection.

Sea control may be defined as the ability of a maritime force to be able to assert total dominance in the common medium of communication, in sub surface, surface and air domains. This cannot be permanent and global in its ambit as the area and the force requirements are too large for any nation. Hence it has to be temporary and localized as is necessary for the mission and its objectives.

Sea denial is resorted to in an asymmetrical force structure of the adversaries wherein the weaker force employs its assets in denying the continuous and unfettered use of the sea and the environment below and above it, to the adversary in the common area of interest. A submarine is a typical example as an instrument of sea denial.

Power projection is the ability of a maritime force to exert unbearable influence on the adversary both at sea and when needed to influence events ashore by delivering ordnance and personnel to further its objective. It is to be understood that sea control is an intrinsic part of power projection. A CVBG is an instrument of power projection.

During the cold war the main task of the CVBG was to protect the NATO Sea Lanes of Communication (SLOC) in the Atlantic Ocean against the main threat of Soviet submarines. The

Soviet Union did not have CVBGs and focused more on worldwide submarine based operations both in the strategic and maritime operations. It was only later when it had established a basic balance in maritime sphere that it made forays into creating its own carrier force. However, by the time this direction could mature, the cold war ended with the demise or dissolution of the Soviet Union. With this the main threat to Europe having been neutralized the main role of CVBG has now become Power projection as was amply demonstrated in the two Gulf wars and also in the Operation Enduring Freedom. In a more limited sense it was also shown in the Falkland war in 1981. An SSN is an intrinsic part of this force and qualifies as an instrument of sea control as its constituent. However, independently and by itself, it may exercise sea denial more effectively.

Therefore, this debate of the submarine versus the carrier in a manner is convoluted. It depends on the economic and military strengths of a nation and its own perceived role in furtherance of its national interests superimposed on its military interests and imperatives. Power projection, in the absolute scale, is an expensive proposition and only a nation with a strong economy, its geographical expanse, its military imperatives and commensurate status could have the luxury of possessing. To my mind, India is still not in that league as yet.

In our own context, we have our own compulsions. On the strategic front, there is no doubt that we have to develop and maintain a second strike capability especially looking at our threats from the immediate neighbourhood and to the one from the North East especially considering our declared policy of no first use and to have a credible minimum deterrent. India is well on the way to address it with Arihant which is already undergoing sea trials and its follow on in various stages of construction.

We also have to ensure and safeguard the security of our Island territories, which are far removed from the mainland. 95% of our trade moves by the sea. These factors impose on us to possess, though limited in scale, a power projection and sea control capability. The viable possibility of a Two Carrier navy and a force of anti-ship cruise missile equipped submarines, both conventional and nuclear powered, address this need. We already have such a force and steps are being taken to modernize and increase this capability. The 30-year submarine construction plan even though delayed and the recent approval of the Cabinet Committee on Security (CCS) to construct six SSNs , is a step in that direction.

In conclusion, it may be said that there is no clash in the efficacy of a submarine and the Carrier. Each has its defined and role and as seen in the composition of a CVBG, the roles are complementary. The fundamental question is the type of threat and the maritime role that is required of each in a definite given strategic, tactical and geographical context and the optimum manner in which it can be addressed. It is not 'this or that' but 'this and that' in a defined context.

By **CMDE Arun Kumar** (Retd.)

# SUBMARINE RESCUE

*"Of all the branches of men in the forces there is none which shows more devotion and faces grimmer perils than the submarine."*
**Sir Winston S. Churchill**

What goes up always comes down, but what goes down may not always come up. This is true for the submarines considering the treacherous nature of the underwater environment. In the event of an accident, the submarine crew is forced to abandon the submarine to reach the surface.

Surfacing from depths is fraught with dangers such as cold, marine life attacks and high pressure. Breathing becomes difficult, and it is vital to provide the correct gaseous composition to enable them to continue breathing during ascent.

Rescue from a stricken sunken submarine is a highly complex process due to the nature of wreckage, availability of facilities and the time-lapse, as seen during the Kursk submarine disaster and INS Sindhurakshak explosion. To escape from a submarine, the submariners have to be rigorously trained and mentally prepared, and the escape drills must be followed meticulously.

The submarines come with some crew safety features, but a substitute life support system is required in the case of a fatal accident.

There are two methods of escape from a submarine, the self-escape and assisted method.

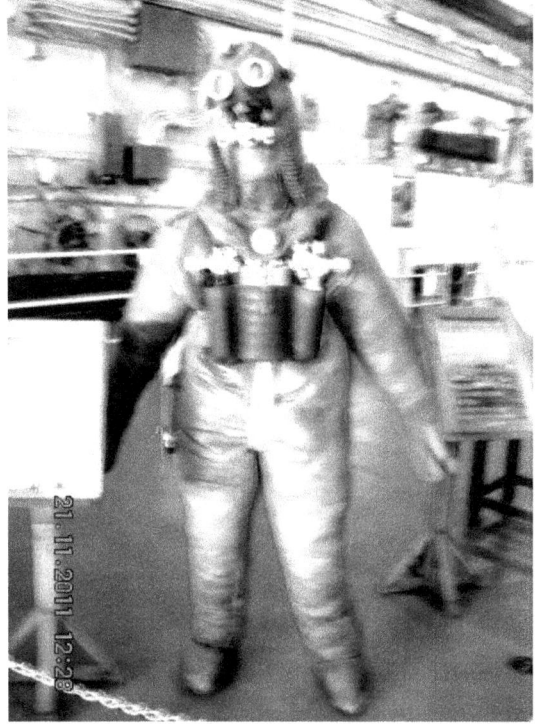

Submarine escapee in the hydrosuit with the breathing apparatus ready for escape. Image: Joseph P. Chacko

## Self-Escape

The self-escape can be undertaken from a sunken or a disabled submarine up to a depth of 100m. Before setting up escape training facilities at the submarine training school INS Satavahana the navy did not possess the facility to conduct escape training in simulated conditions, and the crew had to do it on board the submarines through the torpedo tube in the dry method.

The complete facilities for self-escape were set up at Satavahana in 1974. The navy now has a full-fledged escape facility capable of conducting torpedo escape and tower escape training. When it was set up, the Indian Navy was the only navy on this side of the Suez canal to have a 30m escape tower called Tower of Confidence. The tower also has a 10 m escape stage if the tower is not filled up to 30m.

A diving Pool is available in Satavahana, where the submarine crew is initially given familiarisation training with the Submarine Escape Suit (SES) and the self-contained breathing apparatus (IDA 59) before graduating to the tube and tower escape. Satavahana has three wings viz; the Administrative, Submarine training wing and the Escape Training School (ETS).

For self-escape, a vital piece of equipment is SES. The complete escape set includes the breathing apparatus IDA 59 and the hydro suit called ISP 6. The initials ISP are the abbreviation of the Russian words for the individual escape equipment. The hydro suit protects the wearer from hypothermia and reptile bites and also imparts vertical posture during ascent with the help of metal soles in the boots. It also has a facility to keep the escapee supine (lying with the face-up) using finger bottles provided in the thigh region. These air bottles inflate the lower and upper portions of the hydro suit after the escapee has surfaced. The hydro suit has two sections, the spinal section and the pulmonary section. A breathing bag is an annulus rubber bag worn round the neck and connected to the hydro suit breathing track at the mouth with a swivel arrangement. The breathing bag caters for the breathing needs of the submariner throughout the ascent duration. This bag is fitted with various valves like demand valve, pressure release safety valve, valve box, canister, oxygen and mixture reducers fitted onto the bottles. A breathing bag provides breathing gases of varying compositions depending on the depths with the help of mixture and oxygen reducers. In cold climates, woollen clothing is worn inside. This woollen clothing is also part of the individual escape suit. While escaping from the submarine, the mixture cylinder fitted with a depth compensated reducer and the demand valve provides the requisite gas mixture for breathing on demand up to a depth of 68 m. Between 68-45 m depth, the oxygen cylinder fitted with a hermetically-sealed reducer starts to provide oxygen at preset rates independent of demand up to the surface.

Each individual is assigned his set, and it is located near his action post. Each crew member must know where his suit, which is numbered, is stored in the sub.

The breathing sets IDA 59 may also be used for damage control and firefighting on board. It can also be used for minor repair works on the submarine hull underwater.

It is of paramount importance that the components be periodically evaluated for their functional intactness without actually putting the equipment into the water. Defence Bioengineering and Electromedical Laboratory (DEBEL), a Defence Research and Development Organisation unit, has developed and supplied the test facilities to the navy.

The concept of Free escape was first validated from INS Sindhuvir. INS Karanj conducted maiden escape from torpedo tubes.

In the kilo class submarine, each crew member has a personal breathing apparatus enough to last 10 minutes as a first measure in damage control till more deliberate measures with IDA sets could be taken. The older Charlie-I class Chakra, too, had the same procedure.

For self-escape, all submarines have certain compartments designated as escape compartments. In the Foxtrot class and the Kilo Class, these are the Fore-end (1st), control Room (3rd) and the Aft end. The hatches of the escape compartment are tested to $10Kg/cm2$. Thus, these compartments can be pressurised to 100 mts or more if there is pressure inside the submarine due to damage. If the pressure in these compartments is normal, the escapees are pressurised to the outside depth prior to escape.

The free ascent in a self-escape is permitted up to a depth of 30 mts. Deeper than that and upto 100 mts, the escapee is required to make a controlled ascent to avoid the danger of Pulmonary Barotrauma and Nitrogen Sickness or Bends as is commonly known. To facilitate this, each escape compartment is provided with a buoy rope coiled around a wooden buoy marked in orange luminescent colour. The rope is slightly more than 100mts. It has knots marked at various stages of ascent, usually three, at which the escapee must make a stop during ascent to decompress. The stages are marked with one, two or three knots to indicate the stage. The time required to stop at each stage is intimated to the escapee prior to leaving the Compartment. The first escapee carries this buoy rope and hooks it on the ring just outside the escape hatch/torpedo tube, and releases the same. Each escapee also clasps onto the buoy rope with a clasp provided on his escape suit and commences ascent. At the stage for stop he spends the time needed to decompress. The time is calculated by counting his respirations. A minute for 18 respirations. On surfacing, he inflates the lower section of his Hydrosuit to float in a supine position and the upper section is inflated and then changes over breathing from set to atmosphere, till recovered by the surface rescue team. Apart from enabling a controlled ascent, a distinct advantage of the buoy rope is that the escapees surface at one point, making it easier for the surface rescue team to take them on the rescue ship.

Pic: Overhead view of HDW - 1550/ Sishumar class Rescue pod. Credits : Naval Forces, 1986, Vol 7.

The Shishumar class has an integrated escape sphere with 8 hours of oxygen supply that can carry the full crew of 40 personnel and withstand pressure as great as that can be withstood by the submarine's pressure hull. The crew can enter the module from the forward and aft sections. The sphere is then released from the sub and then comes to the surface. The Akula II, too, has a similar facility. The capsule or the 'rescue sphere' is released from the vessel's bridge in the event of an emergency and can accommodate the entire crew.

On board the rescue ship, which is a diving support vessel, the escapee is checked for his physical condition and administered recompression and controlled decompression as needed.

## Assisted Escape

The navy commissioned an 800-tonne Soviet-built submarine Rescue Vessel INS Nistar in 1971 and based it at Visakhapatnam. It was bought from the reserve stock of the Soviet navy in 1969. The ship was Almaz Central Marine Design Bureau designed Prut-class (Type 527/527m) universal rescue vessel constructed in the 1960s. The ship had the capability to rescue the crew from a disabled submarine from deep depths of 500 meters using a 'rescue bell'. The 1950s vintage soviet built SK-57 diving bell can undertake both the dry and wet method of escape from a sunken submarine and rescue up to 8 people in a single dive. The diving bell and submarine rescue chamber were located on the port side, and mooring buoys were behind the mast. Nistar conducted the diving operation on the Pakistan Navy submarine Ghazi, which sank outside Visakhapatnam harbour in December 1971. From 1972 onwards, Nistar helped train divers to meet the navy's urgent need for Deep Divers and Clearance Divers.

In the mid-1980s, the navy began looking to replace ageing Nistar and evaluated the European Submarine rescue Vessels for suitability in Indian conditions. During the process, the navy also studied the utilization of the U.S. air portable Deep Sea Submergence Vessel.

The naval plans for acquiring Deep Sea Rescue Vessels (DSRV) were postponed due to a lack of funds during the drought in 1987. Around the same time, an MDL built Diving Platform Vessel meant to support ONGC's offshore oil exploration work was available for disposal. The vessel had a dynamic positioning facility and a recompression chamber. The navy took the vessel on dry lease in June 1989 with an option for purchase at a later date. The ship was modified and fitted with the diving system and other equipment removed from the Nistar, decommissioned on $3^{rd}$ November 1989. The purchase option was invoked in March 1995, and the vessel was formally re-commissioned on $15^{th}$ September 1995 as INS Nireekshak. The ship was designated for submarine rescue and saturation diving training. The ship is fitted with a Kongsberg ADP-503 Mk II dynamic positioning system.

In late 1989 under the command of Cdr Philipose, Nireekshak conducted its first dry mating of the rescue bell with INS Sindhuraj which Cdr Arun Kumar commanded. The dry mating was held in the harbour as a first step before trying the same at sea. The bell remained mated with the aft escape hatch of the submarine, which was underwater for 16 hours to test the water-tightness of the bell. The first wet testing for the bell was conducted with INS Vaghsheer off Goa on 5 May 1992 at 45 meters.

On its own, India has limited rescue capability wherein eight personnel at a time can be rescued from a distressed submarine. So in March 1997, the Indian Government sanctioned US $ 288,008 for a submarine interim rescue facility tie-up between the Indian Navy and the United States Navy (U.S.N). In April 1997, the Indian Navy accepted a Letter of Offer and Acceptance (LOA) from the U.S.N. The LOA provided a site survey for Submarine Rescue Service and the supply and installation of holding devices required for mating the DSRV and Submarine Rescue Chamber (SRC) with Indian submarines. The LOA recommended a survey in two phases. The first phase included a site survey, analysis of the subs and facilities of the Indian Navy to ensure rescue operation success. The second phase included developing a separate case to support the actual rescue operation.

In 1997 a U.S.N team evaluated the three submarine classes and airports to use its Submarine rescue Vessel Fly Away kit (SRKF). After the initial survey report in January 1998, the Indian Navy addressed the minor deficiencies. The Indian Navy submitted the status report after four years in January 2002 conveying the non-availability of materials and technology for fitment and welding of Padeyes ( Holding device for securing the DSRV to the submarine) on the escape hatch of the subs.

Subsequently, in February 2004, the Government of India sanctioned an additional amount of US $ 446,435, expanding the scope of the first Phase of LOA to include fitting and installation of supply support items. The LOA of April 1997 was thus amended and validated in March 2004, increasing the project's cost to USD 734,443. The payments were to be made on a quarterly basis, with the final settlement of USD 113,853 scheduled for March 2005. Though the Indian Navy was aware of the poor progress and needed to link at least the future payments with proper milestones, the entire amount was paid by April 2005.

After a meeting held between the Indian Navy and U.S.N in October 2006, the U.S.N agreed to provide its qualified technical team to install Padeyes on the first submarine and to train the Indian Naval welders to install Padeyes on the rest of the submarines.

The Indian Navy welders were accordingly trained in November 2006. In June 2007, the Indian Navy sought the requirement of welding rods to complete the fitment process, for which an additional amount of US$ 9,900 was paid to the U.S.N. The Indian Navy received the additional rods in August 2008.

As per the rescue procedure, the DSRV will be stationed with the U.S.N and in the event of an accident, will be transported to the nearest seaport or airport, then to a mother ship to reach the rescue site.

The nominal response time is 72 hours from the time the DSRV is lifted from its location to reach the rescue site and with the capability of rescuing up to a depth of 610 meters.

A February 2006 U.S Embassy classified document available on WikiLeaks website states that U.S.N had provided standby submarine rescue services for the President of India's planned ride and dive onboard an Indian submarine during the Presidential Fleet Review. Admiral Arun Prakash was quoted as saying that he was very impressed with the speed of the response from the U.S Navy and grateful for the support.

In 2000 the CCS approved to acquire two DSRV systems. Two vendors were short listed after a limited global tender involving ROE (Sweden), Ocean Works (Canada), Perry Slingsby (UK), and two Italian firms. The Swedish and the ROE bid did not include a Q bid (price/Commercial bid) in their proposal hence were ruled out. Both the Italian firms were also rejected before the technical evaluation criteria stage itself as their bids did not meet the first mandatory part of the Request For Proposal. Another Italian company was considered later, but its bid was rejected as it failed to meet the quality requirements. Negotiations with Perry Slingsby and Ocean Works were completed in 2006, and the latter won the tender. However, during the process for discussions with the Price Negotiations Committee (PNC) the tender was cancelled.

In July 2010, the navy sent out Request For Information (RFI) for two large submarine support vessels (or Diving Support Vessel (DSV)) to be built in an Indian yard and equipped with two imported DSRVs. As per the RFI, the Indian Navy is looking for two new 3000-ton diving support vessels with 400-sqm deck space for housing a DSRV and associated gear. The vessels are to be equipped with a helicopter deck without a hangar, accommodation, boats, recompression chambers and diving bells for rescue up to 300-m for 2-3 men with a moon pool. A global tender for 2/3 DSVs is likely to be issued in the near future.

A fresh tender was floated in December 2010 to

procure two kits of free-swimming deep submergence rescue vessels (DSRV) and associated equipment for operation from DSV's or mother ships. The tender asked for bids from firms that have designed and constructed a modern free swimming DSRV that is currently in service with any navy or undergoing sea trials. The final date for submissions was 17$^{th}$ January 2011. One of the parameters the Indian Navy is looking for is a continuous operation for 72 hrs (Frontier India, 16$^{th}$ December 2010).

Between 19$^{th}$ October to 13$^{th}$ November 2012, the Indian Navy and U.S.N's Undersea Rescue Command (URC) conducted exercise INDIAEX 2012, a bilateral exercise designed to demonstrate cooperation between the U.S. submarine rescue system and Indian submarines. It was the first time exercise for ascertaining the compatibility of a U.S. Navy Submarine Rescue Diving and Recompression System (SRDRS) with the Indian Navy submarines. Five Indian submarines participated in the drill. U.S.N press release dated 03 December 2012 states, "They performed submerged, "open hatch" operations over four days, including one day where URC was able to conduct operations with two different submarines in the same day - an accomplishment never attained before. The URC transferred and rescued 158 people from these five Indian Navy submarines." SRDRS fielded its rescue module FALCON, the tethered, remotely-operated Pressurized Rescue Module (PRM). The exercise demonstrated the full deployability of URC's Submarine Rescue Diving and Recompression System.

By 2013, the Indian Navy was also looking for submarine rescue Bell. On 26th August 2013, the

Hindu reported, "A week before INS Sindhurakshak went down, the government took the first step towards purchasing a system to rescue submariners trapped underwater. The Defence Ministry issued an RFI for a 'Submarine Rescue Bell System with launch and recovery system (LARS) on 06 August. The RFI asked vendors to furnish the Navy's Directorate of Special Operations and Diving with information by 10th September. Responses were invited only from Original Equipment Manufacturers (OEM) / authorised vendors and government-sponsored export agencies. Principal components of the equipment sought to be procured were a submarine rescue bell for 12 men, LARS, associated life support systems and a locator system. The system was to be fitted onboard the Navy's submarine rescue vessel.

On 10th September 2014, Janes reported, "The Indian Navy (IN) has shortlisted the UK's James Fisher Defence (JFD) to supply it with two 30-ton deep submergence rescue vehicles (DSRV's) for about INR 4 billion (USD 66.66 million). IN officials told IHS Jane's on 9 September that a DSRV offered by JFD was recently selected over a Russian vessel after emerging as L1, or the lowest bidder, after user evaluation and trials. They said the Ministry of Defence would sign a contract over the next 6-8 months following price negotiations with JFD."

The Indian Navy plans to deploy one Submarine Rescue Vessel each on both coasts.

# AUTONOMOUS UNDERWATER VEHICLES

Quick to adopt, the navy has already floated a tender for 10 Autonomous Underwater Vehicles (AUV) with flexible payloads. The variable payloads expected to be carried include high definition sonars and underwater cameras for reconnaissance of the sea bed, including oceanographic survey and specialised mapping.

> AUV is defined as programmable, robotic vehicles that, depending on their design, can drift, drive, or glide through the ocean without real-time control by human operators.

AUV's are being developed within India at the Naval Science & Technological Laboratory (NSTL) in Visakhapatnam to cater to the naval requirements. Currently, the NSTL is wrapping up the user trials of its first offering, dubbed AUV1. AUV1 is a 1.5 ton flat fish hydrodynamic shaped remotely operated vehicle that can be used for intelligence collection, search, surveillance and weapon delivery. The four-meter long and 1.4-metre wide submersible can travel about 4 knots at depths of up to 400 meters. It is designed to carry a 500 Kg payload, including passive sonar and electro-optical sensors.

In addition to the AUV1 project, the NSTL is also developing a range of AUVs for a variety of roles, ranging from handhelds to 12-ton capacity.

In the 12 ton category, NSTL is exploring a

project to create AUV's meant to be used as 'submadrones'. The project is classified and falls under the Autonomous Sea Vehicle programme. The concept is similar to the U.S. Navy's Manta Unmanned Underwater Vehicle Programme.

Another DRDO unit, the Research & Development Establishment (Engineers), Pune, has developed a Launch & Recovery System for the AUVs. The system consists of a ship-independent Launch & Recovery system capable of launching the AUV at the required depth.

DRDO AUV Model on display

# SUBMARINE COMMAND STRUCTURE

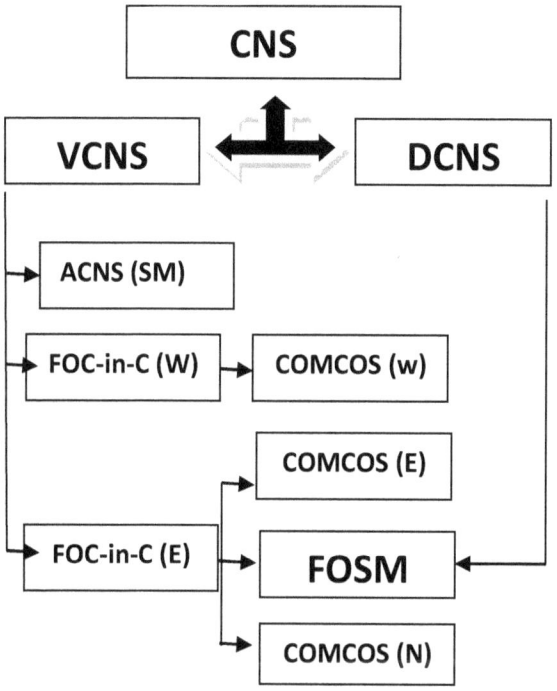

At Naval Head Quarter Level, the Chief Of Naval Staff (CNS) has four staff Officers. Vice Chief of Naval Staff (VCNS) and Deputy Chief of Naval Staff (DCNS) are two among them and are connected with submarines in the navy. The chain of command for various positions are given below.

**DCNS** - FOSM (for Line Functions)

**VCNS** – ACNS (SM)

**VCNS -** FOC-in-C (W) - COMCOS (W) - 10 & 12th Sqn (Operational Purposes)

**VCNS -** FOC-in-C (E) -
a) COMCOS (E) - 11th Sqn (Operational Purposes)
b) COMCOS (N) - INS Arihant & INS Chakra (Operational Purposes)

**FOC-in-C E -** FOSM – CO of Submarine Base and CO of Submarine training School (administrative Purposes)

## Detailed Explanation of some key terms

**Assistant Chief of Naval Staff (Submarine)** ACNS(SM) comes under the VCNS in Staff Branch 1. ACNS(SM) was incorporated at the end of 1996 after Admiral Vishnu Bhagwat took over as CNS since he was favourably inclined to the submarine arm. The argument for ACNS (SM) had been put forward since the early 1990s. It was forcefully projected that just as the Aviation had ACNS (Air) who provided a single point contact on Air matters on the staff at NHQ, a similar position for ACNS(SM) was needed at NHQ.

ACNS(SM) was to a staff appointment, whereas Flag Officer Submarine (FOSM) was a field or line function. It was perfectly logical but was resisted by the General Service to deny additional avenues for a Flag Rank. So a compromise was stuck in 1996 wherein the FOSM was also to wear the hat of ACNS(SM) and was to be stationed in Delhi. Subsequently, as the usefulness was felt, the navy had two separate individuals.

However, in 2007 when Nirmal Verma was the VCNS, and Admiral Sureesh Mehta was the CNS, ACNS(SM) position was dissolved. This state continued till 2009. After Admiral Sureesh Mehta's departure, the post of ACNS(SM) was restored.

ACNS (SM) looks after perspective planning and acquisition of submarines for the navy.

**Flag officer in Charge (FOC- in-C ) West** is responsible for Commodore Commanding Submarines West (COMCOS(W)), who is responsible for $10^{th}$ & $12^{th}$ submarine Squadrons.

**FOC-in-C (East)** is responsible for
a) COMCOS (East) $11^{th}$ Squadron
b) FOSM for administrative Purposes.
c) COMCOS (Nuclear) INS Chakra and INS Arihant

**Flag Officer Submarines (FOSM)** is under FOC- in-C (East) only for Administrative purposes. FOSM is the Initiating Officer (IO) for the Commanding Officers (CO's) of Virbahu and Satavahana so far as their Annual Confidential Reports (ACR) are concerned. Both report to FOSM for the training and base functions.

But COMCOS (E), who is also the CO of Virbahu, comes directly under FOC-in-C (E) for operational functions, that is, for operations and deployment of submarines under his charge, i.e., the 11th Submarine Squadrons. Even if the subs exercise with the Fleets, the submarine commander is under the FOC-in-C's operational control. FOSM for line functions is under the Deputy Chief of Naval Staff

(DCNS) at NHQ.

**COMCOS (Nuclear)** is a new post created for operations and deployment of a nuclear submarine fleet and comes under FOC-in-C (E). During 1998 – 1990, when there was only one nuclear submarine, the CO of INS Chakra was also the Captain (Submarines Special Project) (Captain (SMS)) directly under the FOC-in-C (E). Captain (SMS) designation ceases to exist now and has been upgraded with COMCOS (N).

Submarine Towing

# SUBMARINE TRAINING

*" Each of the Dos and Don'ts of Subamrine Operating Procedures are underwritten by the blood of a submariner."*

The submarine arm is a dedicated volunteer arm of the Indian Navy. To earn the coveted submariners Dolphin Badge, the naval personnel must volunteer and pass an aptitude test. Then they have to qualify in the basic submarine course. This consists of 6 months theory phase in INS Satavahana and six months of practical training on a submarine. At the end of this, a candidate has to qualify in a viva board.

The basic submarine course is conducted on the Kilo-class, which is the main bulk of the arm. For SSK and nuclear submarines, a conversion course is conducted for a qualified submariner.

After qualifying in the basic course, officers are appointed on a submarine to obtain a Dived Watch Keeping certificate, after which they are free to be deployed for independent duties on the subs.

For professional and higher rank courses, the submariners are considered with their counterparts in the general service as per merit.

Satavahana is located in the Eastern command and trains submariners for all branches, i.e., weapons, sensors, engineering and electrical, at various levels to man the submarines. The submarine school conducts 90 different types of courses annually. These range from the Basic Submarine Course to the Commanding Officers' Qualifying Course.

Commanding Officers' Qualifying Course is among the most prestigious courses conducted as per the Advanced Training Program (ATP), and the training team has successfully trained around 160 submarine Commanding Officers.

The school imparts training on live equipment and PC based simulations. It has a live machinery bay, Damage Control bay, EKM control Room Simulator, cut sections of important equipment and ESM simulators.

## INDIAN NAVY'S FIRST LADY SUBMARINER - SURG. LT. WAHIDA PRIZM

# SUBMARINE COMMUNICATION

Communication with submarines is generally one way. Messages for the submarines at sea are sent on High Frequency (HF) broadcasts, which the subs receive through their antennae. Earlier, the submarines usually did this during snorting for battery charging. But if the tactical situation does not permit to be at Periscope Depth (PD) the subs have been installed with towed wire antennae. In such a case, the submarine remains deep and trails a towed wire antenna. The buoy is just on the water surface and has an HF antenna to receive signals. In close formations or when cooperating with aircraft, submarines usually communicate on V/UHF, which has limited range. However, for this, the sub has to be at PD.

Very Low Frequency (VLF) wave lengths are long and usually travel along the ground for ranges up to 1000 km. Earlier, the submarines had a fixed antenna on their fins to receive VLF transmissions, but now they do so with the help of towed wire antennae. Nowadays, submarines also have the INMARSAT facility for communication.

But the basic principle remains that the submarines usually do not transmit unless the tactical need is paramount. This usually would be only in case of emergency or the final attack and report in a hostile situation.

In peacetime, the submarines have to transmit their check reports and diving and surfacing signals. The sub has to move itself from the deployment area to the withdrawal area for doing the same.

For VLF communications, the navy maintains a

transmitting station at Tirunelveli known as INS Kattabomman and the details of the facility has been elaborated in the 'Submarine Infrastructure' chapter. A DRDO unit 'Defence Electronics Applications Laboratory' (DEAL), has designed and developed a multi-channel (Minimum-shift keying) MSK-modulator to enhance the VLF communications. This equipment has been installed at the VLF transmitting site, and the modulator has been interfaced with a high power transmitter, and field trials have been conducted. DEAL has also developed a multichannel VLF receiver with MSK demodulation and FEC using Digital Signal Processing (DSP) techniques. The receiver can reception VLF broadcast messages around the world, out at sea at various depths of submarine operation.

Contrary to popular perception, the navy has no Extremely Low-Frequency (ELF) facility. ELF increases the range manifold but requires an extensive area for the antenna, which runs into kilometres in length. There may be plans to go in for this though no one appears to be sure. Although the ELF gives an edge over the VLF communications, it cannot provide ideal capabilities of high data-rate covert transmission and reception at any depth and speed. Hence, new methods using optical communication like the light from the blue-green laser are being worked upon.

The last mode of communication is the Underwater Telephone (UWT). The consort, whether a ship or a submarine, must have a compatible UWT. The navy is replacing its older UWT's with DRDO developed UWT's.

# INS AMBA - SUBMARINE SUPPORT VESSEL

The Soviets supplied the navy with a submarine depot ship INS Amba (A 54) along with the first batch of the Foxtrots. The ship's purpose was to support the submarines at anchorages in the Andaman & Nicobar Island's. The ship could assist in submarine maintenance, repairs, recharge submarine propulsion batteries, prepare submarine torpedoes, impart combat training on simulators to submarine sonar operators and attack teams on the submarine.

Amba had a unique status in the Indian Navy, being the only one of its kind in service ever. Commissioned at Odessa in the Soviet Union on 28th December 1968, Amba was a Soviet Ugra class ship modified for the needs of the Indian Navy. The modifications were for armaments and radar, which was different from the Soviet ships of the same class. It had four 76 mm guns instead of the 57 mm ones on Soviet versions. This brought commonality with equipment on other soviet origin ships of the navy.

At the commissioning, the crew consisted of 18 officers and about 250 sailors under Captain M.R. Schunker.

During the 1971 war, Amba was transferred to Southern Naval command for interruption of Pakistani sea traffic between East and west and contraband control.

The ship contained intrinsic heavy duty repair bays, torpedo workshops, medical facilities and huge accommodation space, which enabled long deployment of the submarines away from the base ports both in the Arabian Sea and Bay of Bengal.

In the 1980s Amba's facilities were upgraded to provide afloat support to 877EKM Sindhughosh Class. A Helo capability was created by strengthening a part of the ships deck.

It had twin shafts and was propelled by diesel-electric engines with a maximum speed of 17 kts. The 76 mm turret guns were fitted at forward and aft in two twin turrets.

After serving 38 years, INS Amba was decommissioned on 16 July 2006 by Eastern Naval Command Flag Officer Commanding-in-Chief Vice-Admiral Sureesh Mehta.

Displacement :
Standard: 6,750 (Tonnes)
Full Load:9,650 (Tonnes)
Dimensions
Length: 141 M
Beam  : 17.6 M
Draught : 7 M
Speed Knots : 17
Complement : 750
Radar:
Primary: Slim Net High-definition air- and surface-search radar on E/F-band.
Fire Control: Two Hawk Screech on I-band
IFF: 2 Nikhram IFF consisting of Square Head and High Pole A.
Navigation: Don-2' or 'Neptune' navigational radar on I-band.
Complement : 400 Personnel

# KEY SUBMARINE BASES AND INFRASTRUCTURE

## East

### INS Virbahu

INS Virbahu, the shore support base for submarines, was commissioned on 19th May 1971, and the 8th Submarine Squadron of the Kalvari (Foxtrot) class submarines was based here. The Commanding Officer Virbahu was designated as the Captain submarines 8th Submarine Squadron. The 11th squadron was formed after the induction of the Sindhughosh class submarines.

The operational control of the two squadrons was placed under Captain Submarines. Due to an increase in the type and number of submarines, the operational authority of Submarine Squadrons was elevated from Captain Submarines to Commodore Submarines in April 1990. Since the appointment of the Commodore Submarines had a command responsibility towards the submarines, the appointment was thus re-christened as Commodore Commanding Submarines (East Coast) (COMCOS (E)) in Jun 1997.

As the Submarine Arm expanded, Virbahu retained the maintenance, operational and logistic matters pertaining to submarines, while the training role was shifted to INS Satavahana, and the Class Authority functions were taken over by the Submarine Headquarters. But the attachment to the old Alma Mater remains, and Virbahu continues to be regarded as the 'Home of the Dolphins' even today.

The COMCOS(E) and Commanding Officer (CO)

Virbahu are one.

**INS Satavahana**
The establishment derives its name from the "SATAVAHANA" dynasty that once ruled the eastern coast of peninsular India (184 BC to 300 AD), and the crest of the establishment contains the motif taken from an old "Satavahana" Coin.

As a part of INS Virbahu, the unit was an integrated training establishment (Circar II) set up on 11 March 1974 for training the officers and sailors for ships and submarines of Soviet origin. INS Satavahana was commissioned on $21^{st}$ December 1974, and in 1986, it converted into an exclusive submarine training establishment.

Till 1999 the administrative control of this unit was exercised by the Flag officer Commanding-in-Chief (F-O-C-in-C) East, whereas the Flag Officer Submarines (FOSM) was responsible for complete submarine training. Since Satavahana was primarily a training base, the functional control of training was assigned to F-O-C-in-C, Southern Naval Command. The F-O-C-in-C retained the administrative control of the unit, Eastern Naval Command and the FOSM provides necessary support to FOC-in-C South for technical aspects of submarine training.

The Category A (CAT A) training establishment is responsible for both theoretical and practical training. It is the only integrated training establishment in the navy, as it carries out training for all branches of officers and sailors of the submarine arm. Training is carried out by the Submarine School (SMS), the Escape Training School (ETS) and the School of Advanced Undersea Warfare (SAUW).

SAUW was established in Dec 2006 inside the premises of Satavahana to train the crew of submarines of nuclear submarines. The training set up for the Scorpene-class and the P 75 (I) of submarines class of submarines are currently being set up.

Satavahana is equipped with training models and simulators to help the submarine squadrons and the repair yards for defect identification and rectification; and possible additions and alterations to the equipment. Satavahana has a 1:5 scale cut out model of Shishumar class and is used for conversion courses.

The school also imparts submarine training to foreign naval officers since 2005 and has trained officers from six nations. Twenty officers from the Republic of South Africa Navy completed their basic Type 209 Submarine Course in 2006.

**Headquarter Submarines - SMHQ**

The SMHQ was created in 1987 when the constitution of Flag Officer Submarines (FOSM) was approved. Virbahu initially performed class authority functions.

The class authority functions broadly deal with submarine arm cadre management, training policy, Formulation of Standard Operating Procedures (SOPs), carrying out operation readiness inspections (ORIs) of submarine squadrons on East and West coasts, formulation of maintenance procedures, the promulgation of Submarine Temporary Memorandums (STM) and Submarine General Memorandums (SGM) which lay down orders on aspects of operations, maintenance and safety procedures, formulation of procedures for task inspections of submarines, etc.

## Project Varsha

Project Varsha is the name for expansion plans' for a base located near Rambilli on the Andhra Pradesh coast, about 50 km from the Eastern Naval Command headquarters at Visakhapatnam. The construction of the base is expected to complete by 2018.

Also called the Naval Alternate Operating Base (NAOB), the futuristic base is planned to have underground pens to protect nuclear submarines from spy satellites and enemy air attacks. The base is being built in two stages. The NAOB Phase I is a massive integrated plan, and NAOB II is an extension. In April 2013, the acquisition of land for the NOAB II hit an environmental clearance problem. The Ministry of Environment and Forests (MoEF) had opposed the diversion of over 600 hectares of reserved forest land, fearing it may affect the area's water table and soil moisture content.

The base has an advantage over western India bases as the deepwater and harbours have a depth of over 10 m.

### INS Kattabomman

INS Kattabomman is the naval Very Low Frequency (VLF) station, providing primary communication for ships and submarines.

Communicating with the submarines had become a challenge after the induction of submarines into the navy. In 1970's, the navy began discussions with Russia and U.S for building a VLF facility.

Between 1979 and 1984, the Continental

Electronics Corp from the U.S and an Indian government-owned company, the Electronics Corporation of India Limited (ECIL), worked out the detailed design, manufacture, site installation and commissioning of the VLF transmitting station in India. Vijayanarayanam, located at Tirunelveli district of the Southern state of Tamilnadu, was selected as the ideal site for the location of the VLF facility.

During the same period, the DRDO designed the antennae fitted in the submarine to receive VLF transmissions.

Designated as Project Skylark, the installation of the VLF Transmitter commenced at Vijayanarayanam in 1987, and the trials were completed by 1989. On 20th October 1990, the VLF Transmitting Station VT1 was commissioned as INS Kattabomman.

Subsequent to the commissioning, the project Skylark continued and five new transmitters were erected by a consortium including the ECIL, National Institute of Oceanography, Goa, the Indian Institute of Technology (IIT) at Chennai and Bangalore and the Defence Electronics Applications Labs, Dehra Dun (also known as the Instruments Research and Development Establishment).

Four transmitters have call signs VTX1, VTX2, VTX3 and VTX4. The fifth VLF transmitter was opened on 31$^{st}$ July 2014. This facility was mistakenly referred as an ELF Facility by some experts. The older VTI is presumed to be shut down.

The VTX3 uses an antenna system consisting of 13 antenna masts of height 276.45 metres and 227.45 metres. There are two circles of masts around a central mast consisting of 6 masts each. The transmitter has the capacity to penetrate seawater to a depth of 8-10 meters.

In 2004, VLF station VTX1 participated in a study by the Centre for Advanced Study in Radio Physics & Electronics at the University of Calcutta and the Department of Physics at Tripura University to find out the effects of Leonid meteor shower on VLF transmissions. The VTX1 station transmitted a VLF signal at 16.3 kHz, and the researchers could continuously record the transmission at a distance of about 2000 km in Calcutta. There was no noticeable variation in signal strength under normal conditions but increased six to seven times during the meteor shower due to extra ionization produced by supersonic meteoroids in the lower ionosphere.

Housed on about 3,500 acres, Kattabomman has Asia's most extensive antenna system for the VLF transmitter.

# West

### INS Vajrabahu

Post commissioning of the Vela class submarines in 1973, the basic infrastructure for operating and maintaining submarines in Bombay was built up. The first accommodation for the submarine crew was a seven stored building that housed the office of the Captain Submarine (SM) of the 9th Submarine Squadron. For some time, the Captain SM of the squadron was also the Commanding Officer of the submarine depot ship, INS Amba. The appointment was subsequently bifurcated as the full-fledged submarine base began functioning in Bombay. As new submarines joined the West Coast, technical, administrative and logistics support facilities were built. The A-14 building near the South Breakwater was inaugurated as Submarine Base Complex (SMBC) on 22$^{nd}$ August 1987. This four-storey building contains the office of the Commodore Submarines (West), all the submarine offices and the Base Workshop. On 01$^{st}$ February 1996, the Submarine Base Complex was commissioned as INS Vajrabahu. The base is now equipped with a Submarine Motion Control Simulator, Attack Simulator and a water tower building containing storehouses for each submarine.

The 12$^{th}$ Submarine Squadron was formed in March 1990, comprising of Kilo-class submarines. The 10$^{th}$ Submarine Squadron was formed in February 1992, comprising of four Shishumar class submarines.

The base also has a non-dieted sickbay and handles the preparation and maintenance of individual escape suits for submarine personnel.

**Karwar Naval Base**
Located on the western coast at Karwar in Karnataka state, the base is expected to be the home of the six P-75 submarines being built.

# Naval Head Quarters

### Directorate of Naval Design (Submarine Design Group) – DND (SDG)

DND (SDG) is the submarine and submersible design arm of the navy. The arm was formed after the naval designers returned from the HDW project in Germany. In addition to the design of underwater platforms, the arm provides end to end design support during project execution. DND (SDG) is also engaged in the indigenous development of equipment and submarine.

The design team comprises of uniformed personnel, civilian officers and staff from naval architecture, engineering and electrical specialisations. The Directorate is organized in functional groups such as hull structures, engineering / electrical systems, weapons & sensors, propulsion systems, configuration control, materials, etc.

DND(SDG) is also closely associated with the modernization programmes of the in-service submarines under the nodal direction of PDSMAQ and overseen by the ACNS(SM).

Submarine Indicator Buoy. Image: Joseph P. Chacko

# DRDO AND SUBMARINE TECHNOLOGIES

The Defence Research and Development Organisation (DRDO), India's sole organisation for military research, has made many important contributions to the submarine-related technologies and processes in India. The most notable process-related achievement of the organisation is Dr. M.V.R Koteswara Rao's study of life inside submarines and a number of projects related to the environment in submarines. He later published a monograph titled 'Environment in Submarines', which dissects the actual prevailing conditions inside the submarine also offered solutions to a variety of problems faced by the submarine crew. A similar study was done with Submarine rations too.

In terms of equipment, the DRDO has developed a host of technologies that have gone into making India's nuclear submarine, the INS Arihant. Many technologies like the Submarine Escape Sets (SES), VLF communication sets, water mist fire control, USHUS sonar, Panchendriya FCS, AIP, equipment health monitoring and others have been already mentioned in the previous chapters.

Other smaller components are developed like carbon-mono-oxide filters, radomes, flank arrays for submarines, vibration damping materials, in situ paints, etc. The DRDO has created a sonar simulator and other complex simulators for training, which are import substitutes. Sagarika SLBM, Brahmos underwater launch systems, anti-torpedo decoy system, sea mines and Takshak torpedo are prime examples for offence and defence.

USHUS Sonar, Panchendriya and the AIP are three outstanding products that need elaboration.

## PANCHENDRIYA

PANCHENDRIYA is the first indigenously developed integrated submarine sonar and tactical fire control system designed which was meant to be fitted onboard Foxtrot class submarines. However, only one such system was installed onboard INS Karanj for evaluation. Since then, the product has become a state-of-the-art system consisting of a passive surveillance sonar, a passive ranging sonar, an intercept sonar, an active sonar and an underwater communication system. Operated in either single or dual operational modes, the sonar presents its vital information on four colour monitors in 13 display formats. The ergonomically designed system can automatically track up to six targets simultaneously.

The sonar is linked to a powerful tactical fire control system, linkages with periscope, radar and a weapon deployment controller. A built-in simulator available with the system is a powerful tool capable of simulating signals as received at the arrays and can be used for training purposes. The system has provision for online fault localization and an off-line checkout facility to test the system's total health.

The Naval Physical & Oceanographic Laboratory (NPOL) has developed the system and is in production for the Kilo-class submarine upgrade and is available on INS Arihant.

## USHUS

USHUS is a submarine sonar developed with active, passive, intercept and Underwater Communication System (UCS) capabilities. It is based on the Soviet MGK 400 sonar installed on Kilos and was also on Chakra (Charlie – I). This system, too, is designed by NOPL and is available on upgraded Kilo-class submarines and INS Arihant. USHUS is under production at Bharat Electronics Limited (BEL) with on transfer-of-technology (TOT) from NPOL. The BEL website has a comprehensive listing of the capabilities of USHUS sonar suite.

**Salient Features**
- Indigenous integrated submarine sonar system to detect, localise and classify underwater submerged and surface targets through passive listening, interception of signals and active transmissions of acoustics signals.
- Both analog and digital external system interface.
- Modular and rugged design with upgradeable performance features
- Powerful Fault Diagnosis System (FDS) with On-line & Off-Line FDFLUser Transparent Automatic Periodic key change.Local and Remote Loop Back tests.
- To ensure easy customization and updation of the encryption algorithm, without requiring change in hardware, the encryption algorithm is implemented using

a judicious combination of high speed processors and Field Programmable Gate Arrays (FPGA's).
- The encryption algorithm used is complex enough to withstand Sophisticated modern day attacks

**Passive Sonar**

- Surveillance in Passive Mode with high search volume
- Automatic detection of multiple Targets
- Performed Beams in azimuth and in three vertical book directions using ASICS
- Post Processor Normalisation and three time constant integration using floating point SHARC Processors
- Colour coded multiparameter video in 20.1 inch Flat Panel DisplayAuto track for six targets
- Lofar, Demon, Classifier and Spectrum Processing for tracked targets
- Color Coded display to identify target threat level
- User friendly MMI

**Active Sonar**

- CW and LFM modes of transmission with three selective pulse widths
- High source levelLow frequency planar transducer array
- Complex demodulation, replica correlation for Doppler and Range estimation

- **Intercept Sonar**
- Early warning long range target detection
- All round coverage in three bands
- FFT, Spectral processing
- Colour coded bearing Vs time water fall display

**Under Water Communication System**
- Multiple mode acoustic communication in dual frequency to meet NATO and other requirements
- VOICE, TELEGRAPH, DATA AND MESSAGE modes of operation
- Three separate elements to cover 120° in Azimuth

**Obstacle Avoidance Sonar**
- High frequency short range sonar
- Rectangular transducer array
- Transmission to cover three sectors of 30° each

## AIP

The fuel cell-based Air Independent Propulsion (AIP) technology has been developed by the Naval Materials Research Laboratory (NMRL). The membrane used in the initial prototype was a porous inorganic with silicon carbide. Similarly, the catalyst was a carbon paper coated with nano platinum particles. The AIP will generate power between 140-220 KVAs.

One of the uniqueness of the Indian design is that

there is no Carbon Dioxide or any other emission into the water. The waste products will be stored in a separate container in slurry form. Since there are no emissions into the water, there are fewer chances of it being detected.

The Indian Fuel Cell AIP effectively addresses two very important challenges, i.e., the storage of reactants and emissions. The metal/alkaline chosen as a reactant and the waste product slurry require very small storage space.

The AIP has been now proven on a land-based prototype. A submarine-based prototype plug weighing nearly 300 tons is now being made.

# OPS BRASSTACKS : WHEN PAKISTAN'S RED SUBMARINES KEPT INDIA'S BLUE NAVY AT BAY

Operation Brasstacks was the code name for the tri-service exercise held from 1986 through early 1987 on the Western front, along the International border, and the unstable Line of Control (LOC) with Pakistan. The Navy and Air Force were included, primarily to glean lessons and include them in the War Book and War Plans, a standard action taken by Operations Directorates. The display of India's conventional superiority via Brasstacks led to Pakistan's 'official' disclosure about possession of Nuclear Bomb via the discredited nuclear scientist AQ Khan. The moving force behind Brasstacks, was the brilliant, computer literate Army Chief Gen Krishnaswami Sundarji, who wanted to test the new concepts of large scale mechanization, mobility, and air support, with newly formed mechanized units. After his retirement, the Sundarji stayed with the author in Singapore and discussed Brasstacks, while clinking glasses.

The other Chiefs were Admiral Ram T. Tahiliani a test pilot, CNS and Chairman Chiefs of Staff Committee (COS); and CAS was ACM Dennis La Fontaine, a fighter pilot. Both regarded it as an Army exercise. This author has described the trio and their contributions as the 'Gung Ho Chiefs' of the period in 'Indians Why We Are, What We Are' (Manas 1998 ISBN 81-7049-080-4 1998).

Prime Minister Mr. Rajiv Gandhi (1984-89), who

was also the Defence Minister, was enthused and along with his Minister of State for Defence and schoolmate Mr. Arun Singh, cleared the war games. Mr. Arun, a Tripos from Cambridge, gave up his job with Reckitt & Colman to help Mr. Rajiv Gandhi after the death of Rajiv's brother Sanjay in an aerobatic plane crash. The duo were to fall out later.

## Brasstack was planned in four phases:-

**Phase 1:** A tabletop map based tri-service exercise in New Delhi with appreciations, planning and execution of war aims in the Thar desert and the Pakistan border desert. The Army planned mechanised forces and heavy armour in large numbers (10,000) with over 400,000 troops. The Indian Navy and Air Force with plans were included in the war game. A Red force replicating Pakistan's three services was formed as a military team to react to Indian moves.

**Phase 2:** Post phase 1, Western Army Command exercised in a sand model exercise.

**Phase 3:** The detailed Ops Orders were put into writing, and umpires were trained and logistics planned.

**Phase 4:** The land exercise with nine divisions that face Pakistan and 10,000 tanks and armoured and mechanized vehicles operated in the Thar desert in Rajasthan and a little North.

## Phase 1 at Army Parade Ground at Palam

Selected Army Commanders from the Army's Western Sector, the Navy's Western Fleet

Commander VAdm S. W. Lakhar a specialist navigator with elements of the Western Air Command of the Indian Air Force took part as the Blue (India) force. The Red Pakistani plans and moves were planned under C-in-C Pakistan nominated Lt Gen V.N. Sharma the Commandant of the Army's College of Combat in Mhow (Military HQ of War). This writer was Director of Naval Intelligence (DNI and earlier DNO) took part as CNS Pakistan Navy.

The Tri-service exercise was conducted in New Delhi in grand style at the sprawling with large tent age as Command HQs in Tabletop mode. A company with U.S collaboration supplied computers and screens with networking with confidential passwords for security. The Red team was provided sketchy intelligence of Indian forces with locations, maps and exercise calculations.

## The Pakistan Navy Plan that Deterred Indian Navy

The Indian Naval (IN) role in Operation Brasstack was to plan attacks on Red ships, submarines and land bases on the coast and conduct amphibious assaults near Red ports and repeat a 1971 attack off Karachi with the newly worked up Kashin/Rajput class with long range missiles and INS Viraat's planes. An amphibious Blue assault group was deployed across the Karachi Division's Korangi Creek in the Indian marshes near Sir Creek border called Harami Nala by smugglers. Lt Gen V.N. Sharma C-in-C (Pakistan) and his team, demanded Red Naval plans in detail, equal to the Army's for his approval.

DNI's team included a submariner and a gunnery officer, who appreciated the Red Navy was inferior except in submarine prowess and the IN would be aggressive, hence Red decided to employ an anti–access preventive defensive classical maritime strategy. Few PAF Mirage /F-16 fighters were nominated to the Red Navy, while Breguet Atlantics were armed with Exocet missiles.

The allotted Daphné submarines equipped with Harpoons were stationed 75 miles ahead of the ships in boxes with mathematical calculations extracted from an old Allied Tactical Publication (ATP 1) and calculated in manner for patrol areas for 88% success of detection, also in mathematical terms called 'Cordon Sanitaire'. When the naval team suggested one aircraft be equipped with a nuclear bomb to be used at sea as a threat if the chips were down to effect a cease, as Pakistan possessed it, Chief Referee DGMT Lt Gen Sunil Rodrigues (later COAS) asked Gen Sharma to leave that to the diplomatic skills of MEA. No senior naval brass attended the rehearsal a day before plans were to be presented, despite invitations.

A large screen with rear projectors with huge maps of the terrain and charts of the Arabian Sea with depths visible to appreciate submarine operations were set up for the final presentation to PM. PM Mr. Rajiv Gandhi arrived driving his own SUV, bands playing. VAdm Lakhar arrived the day before with a sketchy plan and never expected a full scale plan was to be presented. The Red Navy was the first to present.

DNI's submarine officer presented the Cordon

Sanitaire replete with calculations extracted from NATO ATP 1, in hushed silence. When this author went up to present the Red aims and execution, the presentation was stopped short. CNS Tahiliani was seen talking to the PM and MOS Defence. Later it was leant that the CNS told the PM that if the game was played the Indian Navy's strategy and tactics to overcome Red's anti-access plan would become public. Navy's Red and Blue teams were disbanded. However in the DNI a celebration was held how PN kept IN at bay, despite a bottle ( Naval term for admonition) from DCNS VAdm L. Ramdas (later CNS), that the Red team should not have taken the exercise so seriously, it was an Army exercise !

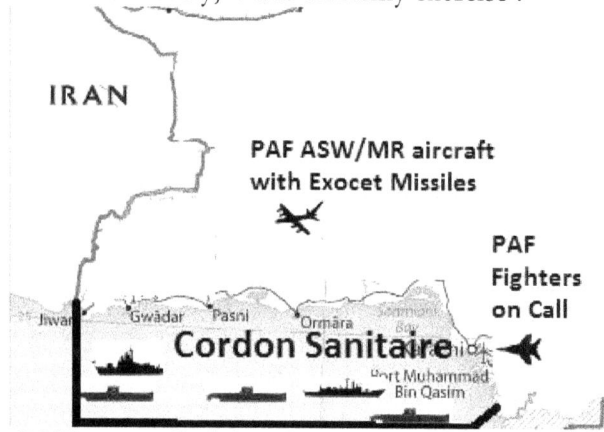

DNI was called in Phase 4 to assist DGMI to defuse the tense situation with Pakistan. Conflicting intelligence both in Pakistan and from RA&W in India emerged that Pakistan had mobilized its reserve GHQ. Brig Zahirul Islam Abbasi, Pakistan's Military Attaché in Delhi spread word that India was seeking war and called on Chairman COS with a highlighted copy of India Today which had published a sensational story. Gen Sundarji refused to accept his call. The reports rattled PM Gandhi and his Cabinet. In later years Abassi (1943-09), as Maj Gen in ISI attempted a coup in Pakistan against Benazir Bhutto and was sentenced.

Military Attaché from Delhi were flown over Rajasthan where the massive tanks formations raising plumes of sand like seen in the Africa Campaign and vehicles were operating, could be viewed from the air, exercising East – West posing no threat to Pakistan. Lunch was served in Bikaner with a Q&A session, bands playing and media invited. A foreign Army attaché remarked. "It's bigger than a NATO exercise, I have taken part in".

As a postscript, Gen Sundarji's ambitions included a national exercise Brass Board after Brasstacks and Checkerboard in the East, to involve most civil agencies like Railways, Shipping and Ministries to activate India's War Book on paper. Due to high cost and the fiasco in Brasstacks with Pakistan, Brass Board was dropped. China's Deng Xiaoping had earlier warned that if Delhi continued to threaten, China would have to "teach India a lesson." The threat had come after General Sundarji conducted Operation Falcon (June – October 1986) in which the Army successfully beat back the Chinese intrusion at Sumdorong Chu, a rivulet flowing north-south in the Thag La triangle, bounded by Bhutan in the west and the Thag La ridge to the north.

By **CMDE Ranjit B. Rai** (Retd.)

# SOME EXCITING MOMENTS IN SUBMARINING

This chapter is a collection of incidents, some humorous ones by **Cmde. Arun Kumar, NM, AVSM (Retd.)**

**The incident on Submarine Day in 1980:**
It was probably our last outing before INS Vagli, which went into a short refit to prepare her for the long passage to Vladivostok for medium refit. She eventually sailed for that place in end September 1980.

I was on board as the Navigator. The serial was a shop window for the families and they were on INS Amba. The diving position was just at the 50 m line as we had a very narrow window of tide to make it back to harbor otherwise we would have to wait till evening which clashed with the Submarine Day reception on Amba.

For readers information, the fuel ballast tanks (FBT) are always flooded with water for diving. They are part of the ten diving and surfacing Main Ballast Tanks (MBT). In long passages or patrols, five FBT's including 2,4,7,8 and 9 can be used to carry additional fuel. If fuels is being carried in them then for diving and surfacing the density difference of fuel and sea water is catered for in the trim calculations. During the passage the fuel from these tanks is used first and the compensation is by sea water. That is why they have emergency flaps and Kingston valves. The no 3 & 10 MBTs do not have Kingston's because of this.

Now back to the incident. The Captain K.S.M. Nair had given specific instructions to the EO

(Equipment operator) and the XO (Executive Officer) to check the opening of the Emergency Flaps physically by going on the casing and check its opening by torch as he had suspected one or two in the aft tanks to be erratic. I was the officer on watch (OOW) on the bridge when the submarine was prepared for sea and the XO turned up late and did not execute the specific instruction of the CO (Commanding Officer). As a result emergency flap of no 7 ballast tank remained shut. If that happens the tank will not flood during the dive as the air will not escape. But a report was made to the CO on arrival that the submarine was ready for sea. When we reached the diving position which was on the 50 m line we carried out a trim dive as per SOP. At that time moment we flooded our centre groups (5&6) MBT which give negative buoyancy, the submarine developed a steep aft angle because the stern did not go down fully as the no 7 MBT did not flood.

I was on the periscope and saw the propeller jutting out of the water. The trim angle was about 25 genres by the bow. We blew and surfaced and recalculated the trim. At that time the Captain asked the XO if he had checked the flaps and he replied in the affirmative. There was no time to check again at sea as Amba was already approaching for the rendezvous. Our job was to dive to Periscope Depth and raise masts one by one as Amba sailed past, fire a Submerged Signal Ejectors (SSE) as a show. It was to be a shop window exercise.

The CO decided that he would dive any way and control the boat by partial flooding of the forward tank and forcing the stern down with speed. We almost succeeded but still developed a steep aft angle and all onboard Amba saw our props jutting out. We were hanging by our 7 ballast tank. On completion we surfaced ( the entire serial was over in about 10 min) and headed back to harbor and just made it before the tide fell below the permitted level to preclude entry into tidal basin. On return the Captain checked the whole episode and then it emerged that his instruction to check the opening of the flaps physically of the FBTs had not been followed by the XO. The XO as a result was written off who otherwise was riding high in the service.

### Traditions of calling on in the service:

We were on INS Chakra. I was the XO and Captain Ravi Games was in command. RAdm Bimu Guha took over as Flag Officer Commanding Eastern Fleet (FOCEF) at Visakhapatnam in Aug 1988. As is customary a RTC (request time convenient to call on you) was made. We were following a summer routine that is secure at 1400. The captain was at home. The reply came 'Your ....... ../Aug 241230. There was no mention of return call time which should have been there. Now the OOW was a 48th course GO (Gunnery Officer, Chakra had a MGO or the missile and gunnery officer). No names. Usually a submariner captain was never given a formal call as returning the same on the boat would be cumbersome to say the least. So this best bet OOW assumed that the reply from FOCEF was inadvertently in error and put WDS (would be delighted to see you) with an apostrophe before 241230. But Obviously RAdm Bimu Guha had thought otherwise and treated Chakra as a capital ship and in my view rightly so. It was an underwater missile cruiser. So the next morning all went as per routine. RNG had come in shining 8As (Uniform No 8A is a formal dress with medal Rigs). At 1215 he left the office for INS Rana which was the Flag Ship. He got back to the office at about 1315 and summoned me. When 1 entered, he looked furious and said 'XO, 1 have never been so embarrassed in my life' and went on to narrate how on reaching Rana's gangway he saw FOCEF and the 1 Gangway staff in No 2s (ceremonial formal dress with full medals) with a ceremonial guard lined up. He had no option but to go on and finish the call. He asked me whether he should render explanation to the Admiral. I told him that their signal reply was in error but there was no point in stretching the issue and it was best to incident. He thought over it and took my advice made sure that the FCO was told in no uncertain terms that he and his staff had gravely erred and that he would be failing in his duty if it was not brought to Admirals notice. I am sure he did because a few years back much after all of us had hung our boots, I had the chance to meet up with Bimu Guha and had laughed over the incident. he was also my fleet commander when I commanded INS Sindhuraj. So calls and return calls have their own idiom. All in a very healthy tradition.

## Unforgettable Instructor

I was part of the crew for Chakra (Charlie I) and we had been deputed to Vladivostok in end Sep 1983. For the first four months we were given a course in Russian language. The Instructors were all ladies and masters in their field. They knew only Russian and, even if had knowledge of other language, would speak to us only in Russian. So in a sense we learn't the language as a child does by associating sounds with visuals. Let me mention here that even though we had been given a crash course in Russian in India for about six months prior to our arrival in Vladivostok, it proved of no value as we could not follow a single spoken word of our instructors due to the nuances of pronunciation. Of course, there were some among us, the senior lot, who had been in the earlier phases of training for the Foxtrot class boats, who were conversant with the language. However, at the end of four months we were subjected to an examination, the level of which could be equated with the Preliminary language examination, either in NDA (National Defence Academy, India) or in a language school. By this time we were competent enough to make conversation and understand the same in Russian. However, to enhance one's vocabulary it was a matter of time and reading. During the language course, we were encouraged to watch TV programmes in Russian. We also had sessions in the Linguaphone cabinets to grasp the nuances of phonetics. Overall, the quality of instruction was excellent. We were now considered ready to receive instructions on the technical subjects related to the nuclear powered submarines, including in nuclear physics, in Russian language.

With the above background, I now come to the main story. We were being taught submarine control and stability by a very experienced and a veteran submarine engineer, with 35 years of submarining to back him, Captain 1st Rank Valerie Ivanovich Selvanov. He was a thorough professional and extremely diligent. During the technical phase, we would draw our notebooks from the secret library and return them on completion of classes during lunch break, redraw them during the study period and again deposit them with the library at the end of it. No written or printed material was allowed to be carried out of the training centre. I must also add that the quality of training we received was of the best quality and I may dare say the best any Indian Naval contingent would have ever received till then or thereafter. The subject itself was such that standards had to be the highest.

During one of the class on submarine control system relating to the control of Aft planes and Trimmers, which control the dive angles of the submarine, Mr Selvanov was explaining the sequence of the electronic signals being generated from the control room to the planes itself, to operate them to the desired angles. There were mainly two regimes, semi-automatic and automatic. While he was at it, I posed him a question to which he did not have a ready answer and said that he would let me know later. The session ended and we broke for the lunch break. Now their instructors were not on the permanent staff of the Training Centre but would be called on temporary duty from their respective stations, on as required basis. They were put up in a hotel 'Primorye' which was also at a distance away from the training centre. After Lunch, they would go back to their hotel and would come the next day as required. After Lunch, I had as usual been in the class room for the self-study period and had forgotten about the question I had posed. At the end of the study period, after returning the books to the secret library, I was on my way to the exit to catch the bus, when Valerie Ivanovich came running after me and said that he had found out the answer and wanted to explain the same to me with the schematic diagram on the transmission sequence of the control signal to the Aft Planes. I had no option but to sit with him and in the bargain missed the bus back home. This meant that later I would have to trudge in the Cold and find my way home on my own. We sat down and he explained the full sequence of the operation both in semi-automatic and Automatic mode. I learn't that he had not even had his lunch and had not gone back to his hotel just to make sure that I did not go away without the question having been answered. It would have been embarrassing for him. I was impressed with his dedication and sincerity. He could have given me a wishy washy answer, but did not and took the pains to study the diagrams and then clarify the issue. We became good friends and later on also when we were practicing the submarine control and emergencies on the simulator, he would make sure that we were thoroughly conversant with the SOPs and was a very hard taskmaster. This was a great lesson for me.

Later when we were in our practical phase of the training on the submarine, the engineer in charge of the ship's Systems including the control surfaces, explained the same sequence to me. I immediately knew that he was wrong and said so. He got a bit offended and said that he had been on the boat for 10 years and knew better. I then suggested to him that we should simulate the signal and then see. When that was done, he was proved wrong and I was right. He asked me as to how I could have been so sure without having been on board to which I replied that Valerie Ivanovich had taught me and that he was never wrong. This was the confidence instructors such as him inspired. I still vividly remember his golden words when putting us through the paces on the simulator which were "Remember these golden words, a minor leak can turn into a major one in seconds. So in case of flooding, immediately plane to Periscope Depth and then examine the damage to control it." To the layman, this action also reduces the external pressure exponentially and thereby reduces the rate of flooding. I must candidly state that it was an honour and a privilege to have been taught by such stalwarts. For me he is an eternally unforgettable character. Much of what I learn't from him on stability, I was able to pass on to the younger generations of submariners as also to General Service officers during the Command examination Board of which I Presided four in succession from 1995-98 in Visakhapatnam.

## Appendicitis Operation At 100m Depth On Board INS Chakra Jan 1988

On the maiden passage of INS Chakra (First one) from Vladivostok to Visakhapatnam in Jan 1988 Surg Lcdr Prakash P Bellubbi,VSM carried out an appendicitis surgery on Licentiate in Marine Engineering (LME) Biswal, which was a historic first in the Indian Navy. The submarine set sail from Vladivostok on the 15th January and was scheduled to arrive Visakhapatnam on 03 Feb. The crew was in very jubilant spirits with the commissioning ceremony having been accomplished with aplomb and being part of a historic first crew of a nuclear powered submarine flying the Indian Flag and ensign. It was the culmination of years of hard work and training and it was natural to be proud of oneself. The passage upto the Southern part of South China Sea was to be in dived state. All seemed to be going well and as per plan. Well into the seventh day LME Biswal reported sick with severe pain in his abdomen. Doc Bellubbi examined him and suspected it to be appendicitis and decided to give conservative treatment and put him under observation.

The condition of the patient took for the worse second day onwards and it became clear that without surgical intervention catastrophic situation may ensue. The issue was discussed with the CO, Capt R.N. Ganesh. We were just abreast of the Northern coast of Philippine Islands (Luzon). Various options of making landfall near a friendly country's port, like Manila, Hanoi, etc were considered but the distances were such as also the time required for obtaining necessary diplomatic clearances precluded such options. It was then suggested to Doc Bellubbi, that it was an occasion for him to put into practice all he had been taught during the training in Vladivostok including surgery for appendix. He was asked to get his team ready. The medical assistant on board was CPO M.A. Karmarkar, a very competent medical assistant. However, just the two of them were not enough to carry out the surgery on board and a team was to be formed up. Usually, on submarines, if a medical officer is not borne on board, the Executive Officer dons the mantle of a doctor. The surgery is to be carried out in the Ward Room, where the main dining table is designated as the operation table with the lights for surgery fitted right above it. In fact these are rigged up when needed and are stored in the sick bay (Medical Officer's cabin).

Doc Bellubbi requested me to be an assistant in the surgery. I as the First Lieutenant fitted in his scheme of things. I told him that I had never seen a person cut up for surgery and was not sure how I would react. I could possibly throw up. Secondly, I had no clue as to what was required of me. He put my fears to rest with his charming persuasion and also said that he would brief me fully with the ailment as also the surgical procedure so that I could assist him with confidence.

Accordingly we formed up the surgical team of three persons; Doc Bellubbi, Karmarkar and self. The Coxswain MCPO I. Gajraj Singh Nears and PO(R) Tel Sajjan Singh were also co-opted as a logistics cum Morale boosting duo. This was most essential as the surgery had to be done under local anesthesia because in the absence of a trained anesthetist GA could not have been administered.

Once the decision had been taken we got down to preparing the ward room. All the officers' cabins adjacent to the ward room were vacated, the hatch going down to the sonar instrument space was also sealed and the Ward room and the bulkheads were sanitized. This process took almost a full day. On the D day, the boat was dived to 100m so that there was not even an iota of a chance of surface disturbance affecting the boat. The operation theater was rigged up with all the necessary paraphernalia. The surgery and the logistic team were also sanitized and the patient was laid on the table. A screen made of a sanitized bed sheet was rigged in front of his face so that he could not see his abdomen and Nears sat alongside him to keep his morale going. The entire crew was engaged, apart from their watchkeeping duties, in silent prayers to wish for the success of the entire exercise.

It had been estimated that the operation would be completed in an hour and a half. As the procedure by itself is not complicated. So the ship's company was closed up at relaxed action station just to demonstrate solidarity with the patient and the surgical team. The Captain, who had been deprived the use of his cabin, was alternating between the control room and the second compartment.

At the appointed time, Doc Bellubbi started the surgery. It was the first time when I was to a scalpel in action and to see an abdomen cut open. The initial incision was to be just minimal for Bellubbi to get access to the Large Intestine and feel the appendix to clip it off. Contrary to my fears I felt no emotion when the abdomen was cut and the cut side clipped to prevent blood flow. It was as if the whole thing was a familiar sight to me. I guess the briefings which Bellubbi had given to me were more than effective and had prepared me to the actual act. Nears and Sajjan Singh were constantly talking to Biswal and narrating the stories of his escapades with the nubile girls of Vladivostok with who he may have been frolicking away not so long ago. He was fully conscious but may not have felt the acute pain due to the LA. The duo of Nears and Sajjan kept him entertained with jokes and anecdotes of our stay in Vladivostok.

Doc Bellubbi kept on trying to reach for the appendix but to no avail. He tried everything that he could but success was eluding. Time was ticking away and the envisaged time of an hour and a half had already elapsed but the appendix remained elusive.

Captain Ganesh was pacing up and down the control room. We had to keep injecting the LA as the effect would wear off after a while. It seemed that Nears and Sajjan were also running out of stories. At this juncture, there was a sense of exasperation a decision had to be made for further course of action. Doc Bellubbi even contemplated stitching back the patient. We conferred amongst us and I suggested that stitching back would not solve the problem. Why should not we cut him open a bit more so that the large intestine could be itself brought out and then see where the appendix had decided to hide? It was risky but Bellubbi gathered enough courage and increased the size of the incision and we were able to get a clear access to the large intestine. Needless to add that this caused increased pain to Biswal being under LA only. It was also to his credit ably bolstered by Nears and Sajjan Singh that he bore it with fortitude. Once the large intestine was full extracted, we could see that the appendix instead of extending from the bottom of the large intestine had wound itself into the crevice along the intestine. To remove it was inherently dangerous as even a nick on the intestine would lead to bleeding which could be fatal. I must stand testimony to Doc Bellubbi's calmness, steadiness of hands and total professional application that he managed to remove the appendix, which had already started to turn greenish. Thereafter it was only a matter of time that the patient was stitched up and rolled back into the Doc's cabin for recovery and recuperation. The entire operation had taken about four hours during which Capt Ganesh, I am sure, would have shed a few kilograms. But as they say 'all is well that ends well'. In the ultimate analysis, it was the calmness and the professional application of Doc Bellubbi and CPO M.A. Karmarkar, which carried the day, but most importantly, the courage and the ability to bear excruciating pain, shown by Biswal (patient) that stood out. He had sufficiently recovered to be evacuated to INS Dunagiri by a helo, which had come to escort us for our surfaced passage through the South China Sea and Malacca Straits. Before leaving he told Surg LCdr Bellubbi, "Sir, you have given me a second life." That was the best reward Doc Bellubbi could have asked for. He had created history. Mr. Rajiv Gandhi, Prime Minister, who had come to receive the Submarine on arrival at Visakhapatnam on 03 Feb 1988 made a special mention of this surgery in his welcome speech.

Joseph P. Chacko

# THE SUBMARINE ARM COMES OF AGE

## A Peep Into the Past

Admiral S.N. Kohli, then CNS, visited Visakhapatnam in Dec 1974, to commission INS Satavahana (21 Dec' 74), which till then functioned as Integrated Technical Training Establishment (ITTE), mainly focusing on Russian acquisitions, in particular the Petya class corvettes and the Foxtrot class submarines. The thirteenth Basic Submarine Course was underway at that time. Later, in his interaction with the officers, the CNS outlined his plans for a massive expansion of the Navy, which included the proposed acquisitions of SNFs, SNRs, SNMs and eight additional modernized AK boats of the Prachand class. I wonder why these boats had not been re-christened as SN boats? To the uninitiated, the prefix SN signified the CNS's initials as it was during his tenure that these acquisitions had been given the go-ahead. One of the officers undergoing the course gathered enough courage to pop the question to the CNS " Sir, what about submarines?" The CNS shot back, "Aren't eight enough?" That just about summed up the perspective of the highest Naval leadership in regard to the Submarine Arm. I may dare say that in the General Service, the submarines were (in the Seventies) perceived mainly as ASW work up platforms. The Fleet Exercise Programmes were tailored to meet that aim. That mindset, to my mind, was a legacy of the Royal Navy, whose operational philosophy we had inherited.

It may be recalled that the Submarine Arm formally came into being on 08 Dec 1967, with the commissioning of INS Kalvari, at Riga in the then USSR. During the next seven years, seven more boats (3X Kalvari class and 4X Vela class) were commissioned into the Navy, thus making a total of eight. The last to be inducted was INS Vaghsheer on the 26 Dec 1974.

**Back To The Present**

On 06 Sep 2005, The Cabinet Committee on Security (CCS) gave its approval to Project 75 (P75), under which six submarines of the Scorpene design are to be constructed in series at Mazagon Docks Ltd (MDL), Mumbai. This would be the first time that we would be undertaking the construction of subs in series indigenously. Our earlier assay in this regard was mainly assembly of CKD kits, in respect of the Shishumar class SSKs ( Shalki & Shankul). Also noteworthy is that this time round, we have been able to obtain a total transfer of Design and Build technology much more in content than was the case in the HDW SSK project. Of course, we had trained our design, yard, overseeing and inspection teams in the earlier missive, and that experience should facilitate the absorption of the total TOT in the present case.

The Go-ahead for P75 is a very significant milestone in the evolution of the Submarine Arm. This would truly transform us into a submarine building nation. Initially, the Project was started in 1992 to rekindle the assembly line at MDL, set up for the HDW type 1500 ( Shishumar class) in the mid-eighties, and envisaged construction of the $5^{th}$ and the $6^{th}$ SSKs. The Govt approval was finally given in Jan 1997, and commercial negotiations were completed in

Jun,1999. However, for one reason or another the final approval consequent to price negotiations was not forthcoming.

In the meanwhile, in Jul 1999, the Cabinet approved the 30-year Submarine Building Plan to construct submarines indigenously to ensure a stabilized force level of subs, in concert with Indian Industry. P75 is one part of the 30 year plan, and under it, approval was in place for the construction of six boats (Including the two sanctioned in 1997). Since the earlier negotiations for the $5^{th}$ & $6^{th}$ boats had been with the French assistance, the scope was enlarged to six boats of the Scorpene design with Exocet missiles, under the overall Indo-French naval cooperation and commercial negotiations were started after due approval of the CCS in Apr 2001.

The 30-year plan is an ambitious one and, when completed, will truly put India as a frontline nation in submarine building. It will have very beneficial spin-offs for our domestic industry, both in the Public and Private sectors. This is particularly significant since our Private sector is now engaged in a major way in the defence arena. The 30-year plan also ensures an economy of scale that will permit the private sector to make necessary capital investments with an assured return on them.

## A Glimpse into the Consolidation and Growth Period

Time to once again glimpse back into the period of the eighties and the nineties. As earlier mentioned, the Arm had been limited to eight boats in the Seventies, which permitted us to consolidate our operational doctrines and lay down firm Standard Operating

Procedures (SOPs) to be followed by generations to come. The emphasis was on professional skills without any compromise on safety aspects. This ethos deeply ingrained has been the singular reason for the enviable track record of the Arm in regard to safety. Many a time, operational and other pressures were put on the Comsubs / Captain SMs to cut corners for expediency, but they never yielded to their credit. The credo "Submarines are safe till you forget that they can be dangerous" is religiously followed in the Arm.

The Arm took a growth ward graph in the eighties, and between 1986 to 1990, ten boats, two of the Shishumar class and eight of the Kilo-class, were inducted. The indigenously made SSKs (Shalki & Shankul) were inducted in the first half of the Nineties. At the same time, existing Foxtrots were modernised during their medium refits.

The most historic and significant turn for the Arm came on 05 Jan 1988, when the Naval ensign and the Tricolour were hoisted on INS Chakra, a Charlie class SSGN, taken on lease from the erstwhile USSR. The boat remained with us till Jan 1991. It heralded the nuclear sub era in the IN, and I was extremely fortunate to have been part of the commissioning and the de-leasing crew. I know for certain that this exposure gave us deep insights into operating a nuclear boat in technical, staff and infrastructural aspects. With Chakra, we were first introduced to sub-launched missile warfare. Around this time, the Arm was operating four different classes of subs, including an SSGN with equal efficiency, professionalism and aplomb.

## The Dark Decade

In the Nineties, there was once again a lull in the growth, and older Foxtrots were being phased out. The construction line at MDL had also gone idle as further construction of the $5^{th}$ and $6^{th}$ SSKs was kept abeyance in the aftermath of the HDW scandal. In fact, the Bofor's and the HDW scandals took their toll on the defence procurement as a whole and the decade from 1988 to 1997 came to be known as the 'Dark Decade' as no orders for ships/ subs were placed to sustain the force levels needed. The negative consequences of this period will definitely cast their shadow on the Navy for some years to come.

## Resurgence and Onward Growth

Mercifully, light dawned on the powers that be, and towards the end Nineties, shipbuilding orders and acquisition of subs were once again taken up. The thrust, however, was for indigenous efforts particularly, for subs, and after a long wait, the $5^{th}$ and $6^{th}$ SSKs got govt approval in 1997 under P75. To make up for the lost time, two Kilo-class were also contracted for. The tenth boat was to be equipped with the Club missile complex. The case for the 30-year plan was also taken up, and simultaneously cases for modernisations of the SSKs and the Kilos were progressed expeditiously. The Kilos were to be upgraded to missile capability. The SSKs were modernized with upgraded state of the art sensors and equipment. The exercise for up-gradation of weapons and sensors was also initiated. We also progressed and obtained approval to acquire a state of art complete transportable submarine rescue system. This system should be in service in the next couple of years. The strategic action plan for implementation of the 30-year plan was drawn up and got approved by the Dept of Defence Production. Extensive relationships were built with the domestic industries so as to enlist them in the execution of the 30-year plan. I was fortunate to have been at the steering end of all these projects in my five-year tenure at NHQ as PDSMAQ. The teamwork and commitment shown by all concerned, both below and above, including various ACNSs (SM) was remarkable. The aim was to position the Arm as the premier strike arm of the Navy in the new millennium.

Whilst those in the Arm from the junior most to the senior-most at appropriate times and positions contributed to its evolution and growth, which is how as it should be, I must mention two non-submariners, who in my personal opinion, contributed a great deal in the shape the Arm took and will take. As the Director in charge of the Chakra Project (if I may use the term), RAdm Narayan Rao's contribution can never be forgotten. One has just to visit the various facilities created in Visakhapatnam for Chakra's basing to appreciate his achievements. VAdm Jacob, who was the VCNS (1998-2001), was largely responsible for the future shape of the Arm. His support was total in all aspects, including in funding such large value projects. During his tenure, the Navy switched to Programme-based budgeting, which found favour with the Govt. He ensured that all roadblocks in the ministry were adequately tackled. This is by no means to forget many other senior functionaries who all contributed in large measures.

By **Cmde. Arun Kumar, NM, AVSM (Retd.) (2005)**

Joseph P. Chacko

# FUTURE OF INDIAN NAVAL SUBMARINES

The future of submarines in the Indian naval service is expected to follow the worldwide trend in technology and deployment. The navy has now begun adopting the entire spectrum of submarine type availability. Once the backbone of the Indian naval underwater fighting capability, the conventional shallow and deep water submarines are being augmented with nuclear ballistic missile submarines and smaller midgets. The plans to induct the AUV's are also in trend with the evolution and use of smaller, autonomous, modular and unmanned vehicles to perform missions under the sea.

Six key trends are expected to determine the creation, selection, and deployment of submarines in the Indian naval service in the future. These include 1) Range 2) Threat Appreciation Matrix 3) Automation 4) Propulsion 5) Armaments and 6) Technology availability.

**Range:** One of the important considerations for submarine selection is the radius of operation. When the Indian Navy was considering the submarine arm in the 1960s, one of the criteria for selecting the submarine was assumed patrol of one week's passage time or 1500 miles from base. A six-week patrol cycle was calculated for the deployment of the subs. VAdm Hiranandani states in the book Blueprint to Bluewater, "the navy calculated that two week's patrol and one week for return accounting for six weeks normal operating cycle was sufficient to reach any area across the Bay of Bengal or the Arabian Sea."

Today, a typical patrol duration is 20 days. The time for passage to and fro is two weeks. One week is kept reserve for breakdowns or in withdrawal areas for tactical reasons.

Initially, the submarines were required to have minimum endurance to reach Bab -el-Mandeb / Straits of Hormuz in the west and Malacca Straits in the east. All conventional naval submarines ranging from Foxtrot, Kilo, Shishumar to Scorpene have an endurance range in snort cum dived regime in 8000 - 11000 nautical miles.

The conventional Diesel-Electric boats are not constrained by their propulsion system but by the fuel, freshwater storage, distilled water and rations. Most ocean-going conventional submarines are designed for an autonomous patrol of 45 days endurance.

Nuclear submarines have an unlimited range, subject to the availability of food and human factors.

**Threat Appreciation Matrix:** The threat perception in choosing the conventional submarines is based on the appreciation of the anti-submarine capabilities of the likely adversaries, their force levels and the enemy's range of operations.

One interesting development is the rekindling of the naval interest in midget submarines for threats nearer home, which was once not seen as necessary. In addition to midget submarines, the navy is expected to induct two-man swimmer delivery vehicles to protect shore / offshore based high value assets and high-value naval assets on high seas.

The navy is developing SSBNs and SSGN's for strategic and sea control needs.

**Automation:** The availability of manpower for the submarine operations requiring longer duration undersea deployment may be scarce in the future. The crew on the naval Foxtrot submarines were reduced to half their strength of 78 personnel towards 1990's, due to transfers to other conventional and nuclear submarines. To date, the navy struggles to find manpower, especially in the officer cadre.

The induction of women into the submarine service is less of a possibility as they will have to be provided separate living areas inside the space-constrained vessel. Surgeon Lieutenant Wahida Prism Khan, today Surgeon Lieutenant Commander, was the first woman submariner of the Indian Navy, but did not find her way into the hatches of an operationally deployed submarine.

Automation may be a major trend in the future conventional submarines. The P-75 Scorpene submarines employ a crew of just 31 due to high automation levels. Automation is a factor in reducing manpower and therefore increased endurance for the same storage capacities. On the other hand, it also imposes greater stress on maintenance regimes.

**Propulsion:** In terms of a true submarine, it is only the nuclear-powered submarine that qualifies for the nomenclature. The conventional submarines are somewhere between submersibles and an underwater platform. Nuclear powered submarines have the desired endurance, but India can have a limited number of submarines due to the lack of availability of processed nuclear fuel.

The diesel-electric submarines have limitations as

they have to surface at periscope depth for air periodically. During the SMM India (a subsidiary of maritime trade fair SMM Hamburg) hosted event on 4th and 5th April 2012, RAdm D.M. Deshpande, Director General Project – 75 (Scorpenes-2000) at the Naval Headquarters, addressed the challenges for increasing the submerged time of the naval submarines. He mentioned two methods being considered, including long-lasting batteries like the one being planned on Japanese Soryu submarines and the Navy – DRDO fuel cell AIP system under progress.

AIP systems are meant to provide the endurance to the submarines on patrol as they are restricted in power and can generate speeds of only 2-3 knots.

However, there are counter-arguments to the induction of AIP in the submarines. Ex-naval personnel have reservations over the AIP because these systems are virtually negligible for a submarine on an offensive mission close to enemy harbours and have a greater value on a submarine on patrol off its own harbours.

They argue that the AIP's have originated from the German, Swedish navies that operate purely in defensive missions, as is the case with the Japanese navy, which operates submarines with AIP based on the Sterling engines. What is required on submarines designed for operations off enemy waters is a very good battery with greater endurance. At speeds of 2-3 knots, the batteries give an endurance of up to 5 days, whereas AIP gives eight days. Fitment of an AIP section has other consequences on underwater profile, manoeuvrability, radiated noise, and speed.

On offensive missions, there is a preponderant

requirement to manoeuver at higher speeds either to attack or to evade enemy SAUs (Surface and Attack Unit) or ASUA (Air SAU) or a Maritime Reconnaissance aircraft for which power from main batteries is drawn because AIP gives only 2-3 knots. Hence, the use of batteries consequently implies charging them. Therefore the need to have a longer endurance battery and a very good generator to charge them with high currents in a quick time.

The future of propulsion is in nuclear power for strategic and attack submarines and hybrid for fleet boats. For shallow water operations, conventional boats will still be relevant.

**Armaments:** The Indian Navy submarines have come a long way from fielding short-ranged 20 Km – 40 Km torpedoes. Today they feature cruise and ballistic missiles with a greater range. India is on the verge of deploying the 700 km Sagarika/K-15 ballistic missiles on INS Arihant, and the DRDO is developing a K-4 Ballistic Missile with an estimated range of 3000 km.

The submarines are being equipped with anti-ship missiles of ranges varying from 40-299 km to increase their radius of influence. The Brahmos supersonic cruise missile with a 299 km range is available for deployment in the immediate future. It can also fit in the L&T made universal launcher currently installed on INS Arihant. The majority of the Type 877 Kilo Class diesel-electric submarines are equipped with Klub-S system with provisions for 220 Km anti-ship missiles and 275 km land-attack missiles. The Shishumar class is expected to be fitted with UGM-84L Harpoon Block II Encapsulated Missiles with a range of approximately 278 kilometres. Brahmos Hypersonic, Brahmos Lite for torpedo tube launch, and 1000 km Subsonic cruise missile Nirbhay (submarine variant) are expected to be available in the next decade for submarines.

Among torpedoes, the Russian origin submarines may continue to feature TEST-71MKE TV electric homing torpedo with a range up to 40 Kms. The Shishumar and Scorpene submarines may be equipped with either 140 Km range Atlas Elektronik SeaHake mod4 ER or DRDO's submarine-launched heavyweight wire-guided anti-submarine torpedo Takshak with a range of 40 Kms. It is meant for anti-submarine applications up to 400 Meters. In an interview with Frontier India in June 2013, Khalil Rahman, CEO ATLAS ELEKTRONIK India, said his company was willing to share the torpedo technologies with India and is already in talks with DRDO and other companies for the same.

These are important in increasing the radius of influence, and longer-range torpedoes and missiles provide a standoff firing range to the submarines.

**Technology:** This is always relevant as the endeavour improves the efficiency per ton of submarine displacement. It covers the entire gamut of noise, propulsion, control systems, Weapons, combat systems, habitability, micro-climate etc. Technology denial to India is history now. The European designers are now more than willing to part with technologies, as seen during the construction of the Shishumar and Scorpene-class submarines. The P-75(I) will entitle technology transfer from selected European, Russian Japanese or Korean designers.

During SMM India 2012, RAdm Deshpande touched upon submarine indigenisation. He stated that many Indian systems would be incorporated in the P-75 (I) submarines, including a water-cooled propulsion system, switchboards, 415 V NES -607 transformer board, 6.6 KV circuit breaker etc., which have been learnt through the Project 75 project.

It is possible that the DND (SDG) can achieve the capability to design submarines in future without the requirement of verification by consultants from other countries.

The DRDO laboratories have also developed technologies for submarines since the 1970s, and a host of them have found applications in active submarines.

The gestation period, which is normally budgeted for 6-7 years, is also an important factor for writing Qualitative requirements for a submarine. This period is the time taken for construction, trials and commissioning.

# TECHNICAL AND TACTICAL DATA

| KALVARI | CLASS |
|---|---|
| **DISPLACEMENT** (TONNES) | SURFACED 1952, SUBMERGED 2475 |
| **SPEED** (KNOTS) | SURFACED 16, SUBMERGED 15, SNORKELING 9 |
| **RANGE** (MILES) | 20,000 SURFACED @ 8 KNOTS, 11,000 SNORKELING, 380 SUBMERGED @ 2 KNOTS |
| **DIMENSION (FEET)** | 299 X 24 X 20 |
| **CREW** | 75 (8 OFFICERS) |
| **PROPULSION** | 3 X KOLOMNA 2D42M DIESEL ENGINES, 2,000 HP EACH; 3 X ELECTRIC MOTORS - 2 WITH 1,350 HP AND 1 WITH 2,700 HP; 1 X AUXILIARY MOTOR WITH 180 HP; 3 X PROPELLER SHAFTS, EACH WITH 6 BLADED PROPELLERS. |
| **ARMAMENTS** | 10 533MM TORPEDO TUBES WITH 22 SET-65E/SAET-60 TORPEDOES 44 MINES IN LIEU OF TORPEDOES |
| **COUNTERMEASURES** | STOP LIGHT, RADAR WARNING, QUAD LOOP DIRECTIONAL FINDER. |
| **FIRE CONTROL/SONAR** | RADAR - SURFACE: FLAG, RECONNAISSANCE: NAKAT, KHROM-K; SONAR ARTIKA UPGRADED TO MGK200 (KARANJ-PANCHENDRIYA), TULOMA, NOISE DETECTION MG-10M KOLA, INTERCEPT SYSTEM SVET-M |

| VELA | CLASS |
|---|---|
| **DISPLACEMENT** (TONNES) | SURFACED 1952, SUBMERGED 2475 |
| **SPEED** (KNOTS) | SURFACED 16, SUBMERGED 15, SNORKELING 9 |
| **RANGE** (MILES) | 20,000 SURFACED @ 8 KNOTS, 11,000 SNORKELING, 380 SUBMERGED @ 2 KNOTS |
| **DIMENSION (FEET)** | 299 X 24 X 20 |
| **CREW** | 75 (8 OFFICERS) |
| **PROPULSION** | 3 X KOLOMNA 2D42M DIESEL ENGINES, 2,000 HP EACH; 3 X ELECTRIC MOTORS - 2 WITH 1,350 HP AND 1 WITH 2,700 HP; 1 X AUXILIARY MOTOR WITH 180 HP; 3 X PROPELLER SHAFTS, EACH WITH 6 BLADED PROPELLERS. |
| **ARMAMENTS** | 10 533MM TORPEDO TUBES WITH 22 SET-65E/SAET-60 TORPEDOES 44 MINES IN LIEU OF TORPEDOES |
| **COUNTERMEASURES** | STOP LIGHT, RADAR WARNING, QUAD LOOP DIRECTIONAL FINDER. |
| **FIRE CONTROL/SONAR** | RADAR - SURFACE: FLAG, RECONNAISSANCE: NAKAT, KHROM-K; SONAR - MGK-200, TULOMA, NOISE DETECTION MG-10M KOLA, INTERCEPT SYSTEM SVET-M |

| INS CHAKRA | (CHARLIE-I) |
|---|---|
| DISPLACEMENT (TONNES) | SURFACED 3574, SUBMERGED 4430 |
| SPEED (KNOTS) | SURFACED 12, SUBMERGED 26 |
| RANGE (MILES) | UNLIMITED |
| DIMENSION (FEET) | 313.48 X 31.49X25.62 |
| CREW | 86 (23 OFFICERS) |
| PROPULSION | 1 NUCLEAR REACTOR OK-350, 82 MW, 1X18800 HP GTZA-631, 1 FIXED PITCH PROPELLER (ON SOME SUBMARINES (K-87) – 1 FIXED PITCH TANDEM PROPELLER), 2X370 HP ELECTRIC MOTOR, 2 GENERATORS TMVV-2 X 2000 KW, 1 GENERATOR DG-500/1V 500 KW |
| ARMAMENTS | 8X1 LAUNCHERS SM-97 - ANTI-SHIP MISSILES P-40 AMETIST (4K66), 4X 533 MM BOW TORPEDO TUBES (14 TORPEDOES SET-65, SAET-60M, 53-65K), 2 X 400 MM BOW TORPEDO TUBES (4 TORPEDOES SET-40, MGT-2) |
| COUNTERMEASURES | MG-14 «ANABAR» TORPEDO DECOY |
| FIRE CONTROL/SONAR | FCS - LADOGA-P-670 FIRE CONTROL,RADAR - RLK-101 "ALBATROS" OR MRK-50 "KASKAD", RECON RADAR MRP-10M, "KHROM-KM" IFF, SURFACE RADAR "VESLO-P", SONAR - MGK-400, MINE HUNTING MG-519 "ARFA" (ALSO USED TO CHECK THE HEAD SECTOR DURING SURFACING), MG-17, COMBAT INFORMATION CONTROL SYSTEM "BREST", NAVIGATION "SIGMA-670", ESM - MRP 10M |

## SHISHUMAR CLASS

| | |
|---|---|
| DISPLACEMENT (TONNES) | STANDARD 1450, SURFACED 1700, DIVED 1850 |
| SPEED (KNOTS) | SURFACED 11, DIVED 22 |
| RANGE (MILES) | SURFACED 13000 @ 10 KNOTS, SUBMERGED 8000 @ 8 KNOTS |
| DIMENSION (FEET) | 211.2 X 21.3 X 19.7 |
| CREW | 36 (8 OFFICERS) |
| PROPULSION | 4 MTU TYPE 12V493 AZ80 GA31L DIESEL ENGINES, 1 SIEMENS ELECTRIC MOTOR, 1 SHAFT, 4,600 HP (3,400 KW) |
| ARMAMENTS | 8 × 21 IN (533 MM) TORPEDO TUBES, 14 X AEG-SUT MOD-1 WIRE-GUIDED, ACTIVE/PASSIVE HOMING TORPEDO, WITH A 250 KG WARHEAD, WITH RANGE 28 KM AT 23 KNOTS AND 12 KM AT 35 KNOTS, MINES - 24 X EXTERNAL STRAP-ON |
| COUNTERMEASURES | C303 DECOY; ESM: AGRO PHENIX II AR 700 OR KOLL MORGEN SEA SENTRY, ESM -DR 3000 SINGER LIBRASCOPE MKI, RADAR WARNING, CCS 90--1/ISUS SURFACE SEARCH, THOMSON-CSF CALYPSO RADAR AT I-BAND FREQUENCY |
| FIRE CONTROL/SONAR | ATLAS ELEKTRONIK CSU 90 HULL-MOUNTED PASSIVE AND ACTIVE SEARCH-AND-ATTACK SONAR AND FLANK SONAR ARRAYS, THOMSON SINTRA DUUX-5 WITH PASSIVE RANGING & INTERCEPT. |

## SINDHUGHOSH CLASS

| | |
|---|---|
| DISPLACEMENT (TONNES) | SURFACED 2300, DIVED :3100 |
| SPEED (KNOTS) | SURFACED 10, DIVED 17, SNORTING 9 |
| RANGE (MILES) | SURFACED 23000, SUBMERGED 3100 |
| DIMENSION (FEET) | 238 X 32.5 X 21.7 |
| CREW | 53 (13 OFFICERS |
| PROPULSION | 2 MODEL 4-2AA-42M DIESELS; 2 GENERATORS; 1 MOTOR; 1 SHAFT; 2 MT-168 AUXILLIARY MOTORS; 1 ECONOMIC SPEED MOTOR |
| ARMAMENTS | TYPE 53-65 PASSIVE WAKE HOMING TO 19 KM (10.3 N MILES) @ 45 KNOTS; TEST 71/76 ANTI-SUBMARINE, ACTIVE-PASSIVE HOMING TORPEDO - 15 KM @ 40 KT OR 20 KM (@ 25 KT WARHEAD 220 KG. TOTAL OF 18 WEAPONS. WIREGUIDED TORPEDO ON TWO TUBES. 9M36 STRELA-3(SA-N-8) SAM LAUNCHER IN FIN.MINES - 24 DM1 IN LIEU OF TORPEDOES. KLUB MISSILES – ANTI-SHIP AND ANTI LAND. |
| COUNTERMEASURES | SQUID HEAD RADAR WARNING, PORPOISE (INDIGENOUS) |
| FIRE CONTROL/SONAR | FCS - UZWL MVU-119EM TFCS; RADAR- NAVIGATION; ONE MRP-25 (SNOOP TRAY) RADAR I BAND; SONAR- NAVIGATION MGK400, HULL MOUNTED, ACTIVE / PASSIVE SEARCH AND ATTACK; MEDIUM FREQUENCY, MG519; HULL MOUNTED ACTIVE SEARCH; HIGH FREQUENCY. BEING REPLACED BY USHUS SONAR BY BEL. |

## SCORPENE CLASS

| | |
|---|---|
| **DISPLACEMENT (TONNES)** | DIVED 1,668 |
| **SPEED (KNOTS)** | SURFACED 11, DIVED 22 |
| **RANGE (MILES)** | SURFACED 7480 @ 8 KNOTS, SUBMERGED 630 @ 5 KNOTS |
| **DIMENSION (FEET)** | 217.8 X 20.3 X 19 |
| **CREW** | 31 (6 OFFICERS) |
| **PROPULSION** | 4 X MTU 16 V 396 SE84 DIESEL ENGINES, 1 JEUMOUNT (METERS) SCHNEIDER MOTOR, 1 SHAFT |
| **ARMAMENTS** | 6-21 INCHES (533 MM) TUBES |
| **COUNTERMEASURES** | ESM |
| **FIRE CONTROL/SONAR** | FCS - UDS INTERNATIONAL SUBTICS, NAVIGATION - SAGEM; I BAND, SONAR - HULL MOUNTED PASSIVE AND ATTACK - MEDIUM FREQUENCY |

| INS CHAKRA | AKULA-II |
|---|---|
| **DISPLACEMENT** (TONNES) | SURFACED 8450, DIVED 13400 |
| **SPEED** (KNOTS) | DIVED 28.35, SURFACED 10 |
| **RANGE** (MILES) | UNLIMITED |
| **DIMENSION (FEET)** | 113.3 X 13.6 X 9.7 |
| **CREW** | 90 (23 OFFICERS) |
| **PROPULSION** | 1 VM5 NUCLEAR PWR; 190 MW; ONE OK-7 STEAM TURBINE; 43,000 HP(M); 2 RETRACTABLE ELECTRIC PROPULSORS FOR LOW SPEED AND QUIET MANOEUVRING; 750 HP(M) (552 KW); 1 SHAFT; 2 SPINNERS; 1,006 HP (M) (740 KW) |
| **ARMAMENTS** | SLCM/SSM: KLUB S 3M 54E (ANTI-SHIP)/ 3M 14 E (LAND ATTACK), NATO 55-N27, FIRED FROM 21 IN (533MM) TORPEDO TUBES. THE ANTI-SHIP VERSION IS A SEASKIMMER WITH 200 KG WARHEAD, 200 KM RANGE, FLIGHT ALTITUDE OF 15 FT AND SUPERSONIC TERMINAL SPEED (2.9 MACH) IN THE FINAL STAGE. THE LAND ATTACK MISSILE IS INERTIALLY GUIDED, SUBSONIC (0.8 MACH, HAS A RANGE - 275 KM AND A 400-KG WARHEAD. SA-N-10 IGLA M LAUNCHER ON SAIL, 18 MISSILES. TYPE 40 TORPEDO. NOVATOR SS-N-16 STALLION FIRED FROM 100 KMS (54 N MILES); 8X21 IN (533 MM) TUBES. TOTAL OF 40 WEAPON5. |
| **COUNTERMEASURES** | ESM - RIM HAT; INTERCEPT. SURFACE SEARCH - SNOOP PAIR OR SNO HALF WITH BACK-TO-BACKAERIALS ON SAME MAST AS ESM. |

| INS | ARIHANT |
|---|---|
| DISPLACEMENT (TONNES) | 6,000 TONNES (5,900 LONG TONS; 6,600 SHORT TONS) |
| SPEED (KNOTS) | SURFACED 12–15 KNOTS, SUBMERGED 24 KNOTS |
| RANGE (MILES) | UNLIMITED |
| DIMENSION (FEET) | 367 X 49 X 33 |
| CREW | 95 |
| PROPULSION | 80MWE PWR FUELLED BY 40% ENRICHED URANIUM; 1 TURBINE (1,11,000 HP/83 MW), 1 SHAFT, ONE 7 BLADE HIGH-SKEW PROPELLER (ESTIMATED) |
| ARMAMENTS | MISSILES - 12 × K15 SLBM (750 KM RANGE) OR 4 × K-4 SLBM (UNDER DEVELOPMENT) (3500 KM RANGE), TORPEDOES: 6 × 21" (533 MM) TORPEDO TUBES – ESTIMATED 30 CHARGES (TORPEDOES, CRUISE MISSILES OR MINES). |
| COUNTERMEASURES | RAFAEL BROADBAND EXPENDABLE ANTI-TORPEDO COUNTERMEASURES |
| FIRE CONTROL/SONAR | USHUS INTEGRATED SONAR, PANCHENDRIYA SUBMARINE SONAR AND TACTICAL WEAPONS CONTROL SYSTEM WITH ACTIVE, PASSIVE RANGING, SURVEILLANCE AND INTERCEPT SONARSAND UNDERWATER COMMUNICATION SYSTEM. TWIN FLANK-ARRAY SONARS ON HULL. |

# ABBREVIATIONS

AIP - Air Independent Propulsion
ATV - Advanced Technology Vessel
BARC – Bhabha Atomic Research Center
CAG - Comptroller and Auditor General
CDR - Commander
CENTO - Central Treaty Organization
DND (SDG) - Directorate of Naval Design (Submarine Design Group)
CMDE - Commodore
DRDO – Defence Research and Development Organisation
DSRV - Deep Submergence Rescue Vehicle
DTCN - Direction Technique Construction Navale (French)
FOC-in-C (W) - Flag Officer in Command – West
L&T – larser and Toubro Pvt ltd
HAT - Harbour Acceptance Trial
HDW - Howaldtswerke-Deutsche Werft
MDL - Mazagon Dock Limited
MoD - Ministry of Defence
MPM - Mazagon Procured Materials
NATO - North Atlantic Treaty organisation
NHQ - Naval Head Quarters
PMS - Platform Management System
RADM - Rear Admiral
RFI – Request for Information
SAT - Sea Acceptance Trial
SEATO - Southeast Asia Treaty Organization
SLBM – Submarine Launched Ballistic Missile
SOP - Standard Operating Procedure
SSBN - Ship Submersible Ballistic, Nuclear
SSK - Ship Submersible hunter-killer
SSGN - Ship Submersible Guided, Nuclear (Cruise Missile)
TCSF - Thomson-CSF
ToT - Transfer of Technology
TLM – Tube Launched Missile
VADM - Vice Admiral
VLS – Vertical Launch System

Joseph P. Chacko

# INDEX

## SUBMARINES
**ATV/ATVP:** VII, 96, 112, 119 - 125, 132,137, 139 - 142, 144, 149
**ARIDAMAN:** 131 - 133
**ARIHANT:** 5, 8, 86, 119 - 121, 123 - 127, 128 - 134, 137 - 139, 141 - 142, 159, 176, 177, 193 - 195, 228, 238
**CHAKRA**: 46, 99, 104 -106, 108, 109, 114 - 117, 122-23, 128 - 130, 140 - 141, 147, 164, 176 – 178, 195, 207, 208, 212, 221, 233
**CHARLIE 1:** 124, 233
**AKULA :** 7, 8, 110, 112, 115 - 118, 146, 166, 237
**FOXTROT:** 1, 23, 28, 30, 35, 45, 78, 140, 144, 164, 183, 185, 194, 209, 218, 221, 222, 225, 226
**HDW 209 TYPE 1500:** 2, 7, 35 - 40, 43, 45, 51 - 54, 57, 69, 95, 139, 144 - 145, 149 - 150, 165, 191, 219, 223, 237
**IRBIS**: 112, 117
**KALVARI:** 1, 23 - 29, 65, 68, 69, 73, 185, 219, 231
**KARANJ:** 25, 27, 66, 67, 68, 70, 71, 73 - 76, 79 -80, 163, 194, 231
**KHANDERI:** 25 - 27, 68, 73, 140 KURSURA : 25 - 27, 68, 69, 70, 72, 74 – 76,
**PROJECT 75/ P 75:** 51, 57, 59, 63, 67, 148, 219, 230, **PROJECT 75 (INDIA)/P 75 I :** 8, 56, 148 - 152, 187, 226, 229, 230,
**SCORPENE SUBMARINE:** 2, 8, 52, 53, 56 - 65, 67, 145, 146, 148 - 150, 187, 219, 220, 225 - 227, 229, 236
**SINDHUGHOSH :** 45, 46, 48, 81, 84, 184, 185, 235
**SINDHUDHVAJ :** 46 **SINDHURAJ :** 46, 167, 208, 235 **SINDHUVIR :** 46, 163
**SINDHURATNA :** 46, 81, 83 **SINDHUKESARI :** 46 **SINDHUKIRTI :** 46
**SINDHUVIJAY :** 46 **SINDHURAKSHAK :** 46, 47, 80, 82, 134, 160, 172
**SINDHUSHASTRA :** 46 **SHALKI :** 39, 42, 43, 219, 221 **SHANKUL :** 39, 43, 219, 221
**SHANKUSH :** 39, 41, 42
**SHISHUMAR :** 35, 39 - 43, 48, 51, 54, 56, 86, 165, 187, 191, 219, 221, 225, 228, 229, 234
**877EKM/KILO/:** 2, 7, 8, 40, 45 – 49, 55, 82, 85, 86, 103, 113, 116, 134, 146, 164, 179, 180, 184, 191, 194, 195, 216, 221, 222, 225, 228,
**VAGIL:** 30 **VAGIR:** 30 **VAGSHEER :** 30 **VELA :** 28, 30, 81, 88, 190, 219, 232

## SHIPS
**AMBA:** 22, 25, 30, 88, 183, 184, 190, 203 - 205 **NIREEKSHAK:** 167
**NISTAR:** 87, 166, 167

## ESTABLISHMENTS
**DND (SDG):** 48, 51, 54, 191, 192, 230 **HQ SUBMARINES :** 187
**KARWAR NAVAL BASE:** 191 **KATTABOMMAN:** 136, 182, 188, 189
**SATAVAHANA:** 8, 25, 100, 161, 162, 177, 179, 185 − 187, 216, 218, **VARSHA:** 139, 188 **VAJRABAHU:** 42, 190, 191 **VIRBAHU:** 24 - 26, 68, 177, 185, 187
**MAZAGON DOCKS LTD / MDL:** 2, 38, 39, 40, 42, 51, 52, 57- 64, 66, 67, 95, 123, 140, 148, 151, 167, 219, 222,

# ABOUT CMDE ARUN KUMAR (RETD)

The book has been written in consultation with Cmde Arun Kumar (Retd). Cmde Arun has had a distinguished career of 31 years in the Navy. He was commissioned into the Navy on 01 Jul 1973 after graduating from NDA [41st Course]. Soon after obtaining his Watchkeeping certificate, he joined the Submarine Arm in 1975. He topped his submarine course in 1976 and obtained his Dived Watchkeeping Certificate soon thereafter. During his 28 years in submarines, he held various staff and command appointments. He topped his SM COQC(Perishers).

His Commands include two kilo-class subs viz; Sindhuraj & Sindhughosh, Submarine Base Captain and Capt SM 10 ( Sqn captain Shishumar Class), INS Virbahu & COMCOS (E), guided-missile destroyer Rajput, Submarine Training School Satavahana. His last appointment was PDSMAQ at NHQ, where he steered submarine projects of strategic importance to the Arm in particular and the Navy in General. He is a specialist Navigator, wherein he topped the course in 1980. He has also attended the Staff Course at DSSC and the Naval Higher Command Course. He was part of the Commissioning crew as First Lieutenant of IN's first SSGN Chakra and formulated its SOPs. He was decorated twice by the President of India for his devoted and distinguished serviccs with Nao Sena Medal(NM) in 1991 and Ati Vishisht Seva Medal(AVSM) in 2003. He took premature retirement in 2004.

Cmde Arun Kumar, NM receives Ati Vishist Seva Medal (AVSM) from President A.P.J Abdul Kalam.

# ABOUT THE AUTHOR

Joseph P. Chacko is a defence journalist, entrepreneur, and Frontier India publisher, portal publishing news and current affairs. He specializes in defence and strategic affairs. He holds an M.B.A in International Business from the Maharishi University of Management, Iowa, USA. He has co-authored the book Warring Navies – India and Pakistan.

# Get Published with Frontier India

Do you want to get your book or thesis published? You might even want to republish your book which is currently out of print.. Frontier India Technology as a publisher, distributor and retailer of books, offers a complete range of publishing, editorial, and marketing services that helps you as an author to take his or her book to the reader.

Getting your work published is a wish for many for reasons including profit earning, self-satisfaction, popularity and other good reasons. We will offer you choices based on your needs. Get in touch with us at frontierindia@gmail.com.

**Our Recently Published Books include :**

**An Indian Air force Recollects** by Wing Co P.K. Karayi ( Retd.) ISBN: 978-8193005507
**Warring Navies – India and Pakistan** (International Edition) – by Cmde Ranjit B. Rai (Retd.). Joseph P. Chacko. ISBN: 978-8193005545
**Basics of marriage Management** by Walter E Vieira. ISBN: 978-8193005514
**Beat That Exam Fever – Succeed in Examinations** by Walter E Vieira. ISBN: 978-8193005538
**Ordinary Stocks, Extra Ordinary Profits** by Anand S. ISBN: 978-8193005521
**Foxtrots of the Indian Navy** by Cmde P.R Franklin. ISBN: 9788193005576

www.ingramcontent.com/pod-product-compliance
Lightning Source LLC
Chambersburg PA
CBHW060834190426
43197CB00039B/2589